The
2001
New York City
Marathon

United We Run

by

Brian Holdich

By the same author
My Indian Journey
India Revisited

———————————

Published in Great Britain by
Brian's Books (B.W. Holdich),
4 Elm Close,
Market Deeping,
Lincs.
PE6 8JN

ISBN 0 9521017-2-6 (Paperback)
The 2001 New York City Marathon

Printed and bound by Peter Spiegl & Co.,
6 St. George's Street,
Stamford,
Lincolnshire.
PE9 2BL

I dedicate this book to Edna, a longtime sufferer of motor neurone disease, undoubtedly the bravest lady I've ever known, she being my inspiration on this the toughest of all marathons.

Acknowledgments

I cannot overstate my indebtedness to the following people concerned; first my gratitude to Dr. Neil Marshall, my G.P for over 26 years for kindly agreeing to write the foreword to this book; my thanks also to Geoff Chambers and Henry Roberts, two good friends whose comments on reading the proofs before publication I greatly valued; I must also acknowledge my thankfulness to Peter Spiegl & Co., my printers for their usual meticulousness in producing my third book; my appreciation to Lynda Lee-Potter columnist of the Daily Mail newspaper who informed me of the company P.A. Photos, and it was they who supplied me with photographs of the marathon and the so dramatic pictures of the World Trade Centre catastrophe with its massive loss of life; special thanks therefore to P.A. Photos and to Laura Wurzal of that company, whom over the telephone I had many conversations with, she being so helpful and considerate. Also I am extremely grateful to the charity "Get Kids Going" who accepted me to compete in the New York Marathon, and for whom I was proud to raise money for; finally to my wife Kathleen go my heartfelt thanks, who has to put up with her husband's obsession with walking, and of course only she knows the hundreds of hours I took to write this book. I am especially grateful to her.

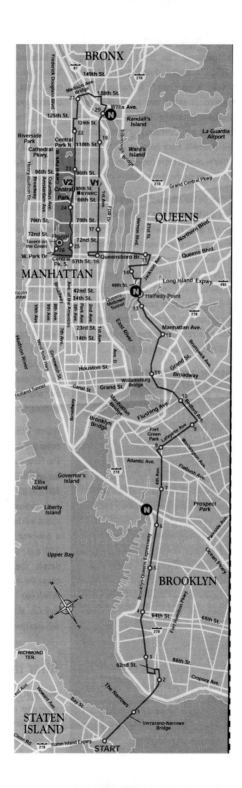

The
Marathon
Route

Foreword
by his Doctor

Those who have read the books that he wrote (1991 and 1996) after each of his two trips to India will already be familiar with Brian's common themes of walking, discovery and charity.

This time, through the eyes of a participant in the 2001 New York marathon he has written an engaging account of another of his adventures abroad. His talent for walking considerable distances and his ability to strike up conversations with strangers are perhaps a happy consequence of the many years when he was working daily 'door to door' visiting his clients. Nevertheless it is a considerable achievement to have walked 26 miles through the streets of New York in one day.

By completing the marathon on November 4th he has, with sponsorship from friends and neighbours, once again fulfilled a personal ambition to raise money for an important charitable cause - on this occasion the charity is 'Get Kids Going'.

Brian's descriptive and down to earth narrative style succeeds because he observes and retains so much detail about the things and the people he sees around him - things which many of us would fail even to notice. Not every writer would include graphic detail about bodily functions, but Brian has done so with good humour! He recalls the little day to day experiences and conversations, often with strangers, which make life so worth living. The reader who has never been to New York will gain many insights into the spirit of 'The Big Apple' in the aftermath of the terrorist attack on September 11th. Those who thought they were already familiar with New York will be surprised by some of the facts revealed in this book. Also revealed is the enormity of the task of organising the New York marathon.

Although he is a walker and not a runner, the emotions

felt before, during and after such a major event must be very similar to those felt by the other participants. Brian has described what went through his mind stage by stage in revealing detail. Of course, as he reminds us, his marathon lasted many hours longer than that of the many runners making it, in a sense, even more of an ordeal (for him).

The unfortunate wear and tear of his ankle joint is not very surprising after all that walking, but may prevent him from competing in marathons in the future. I suspect, however, that Brian will find other ways to test his personal endurance and that he will again adventure abroad and raise funds for lucky charities. Perhaps we can even hope for another enjoyable book to read (in a few years time?)

Dr. Neil Marshall
The Deeping's Practice
Market Deeping
25th July 2002

Contents

Author's Note

"Give my regards to Broadway, Remember me to Herald's Square". Yes, I actually did burst into song as I sung those immortal words made famous by the legendary entertainer Al Jolson. It seemed such an appropriate and natural thing for me to do because here I was in Manhattan and only a few streets away from Broadway and I was being given the freedom of 1st Avenue by the so obliging and smiling New York City traffic cops, who were forever encouraging me on with the so familiar words of "Keep Going Buddy", and were allowing me to walk literally all on my own in the centre of what would normally be a very busy 1st Avenue.

I had trailed behind many thousands of other athletes who like me were participating in the New York City marathon and being a walker it would not have bothered me unduly if I was last because just being there in Manhattan was so very special on such an unforgettable day. Also high on my singing agenda for the day was "Autumn in New York", which also seemed so appropriate as it was the autumn in New York, and when one enters a marathon one will virtually try anything to keep the momentum and concentration going as one strives to overcome endless obstacles, where strangely enough singing helped me enormously as I had at times to draw on all my reserves of energy. Not only physically but mentally too, when it would have been so easy and convenient to have thrown in the towel and given up.

The reason for writing this book is two-fold because it not only gives an insight into the trials and tribulations of a marathon walker, but when I visited Ground Zero I also felt the need to write down what I'd seen with my very own eyes. Something so indescribable that one strives to find the appropriate words for such a murderous assault of preposterous proportions, that the world might never com-pletely recover from, and as you read through this book you will read how I intend to help in some small way.

Chapter One

New York, New York

(So good they named it twice)

New York, New York, so good they named it twice. That indeed is how the song goes. New York City being in New York State is without question one of the great cities of the world, if not the greatest. It's been said that it's a city that never sleeps, which is true because on visiting New York be prepared for a wonderful adventure and a truly magnificent place to visit. It's almost like living in a pressure cooker as one experiences such incredible activity which can at times seem quite overwhelming with such a frenzy of energy and enterprise going on all around one. The streets and avenues are packed with shoppers and excited holiday makers and having visited the city twice inside twelve months, I can categorically state there is an undoubted buzz about New York which I've never experienced in any other city. The city itself is situated on the island of Manhattan and even a non-shopper like myself has to admit that New York is a shoppers' paradise for the ladies of course. The only thing you will require though is plenty of money when one visits this most vibrant of all cities because the department stores are simply the best, Manhattan being the home of Macy's, the biggest department store in the world, shop till you drop at Bloomingdales, Saks, Gucci, Cartier, Versace and not forgetting Tiffany's, made even more famous by the film "Breakfast at Tiffany's", providing you do not expect to see the delectable and delicious Audrey Hepburn sitting there. Sophisticated Fifth Avenue is a must for shoppers to browse through and it's said that anything can be found on those glittering streets. New York has a magnetism all its own and it is also known affectionately as 'The Big Apple'.

New York City at its last census in 1990 had a population of 7.3 million people that is spread over the five boroughs, which are Manhattan, Brooklyn, Queens, The Bronx and Staten Island. New York today represents every race on earth and where I am sure every language is spoken. The name of the Big Apple was popularised in the 1920s and by the 1970s the city began using the name to market tourism and there it stands today a city of canyons of steel where millions of visitors flock to every year. The attractions and charms of New York will intoxicate anyone who is prepared to delve behind all that steel, concrete and glass which we automatically associate with those towering skyscrapers in Manhattan. It would be virtually impossible to see it all in one week because the tourist attractions are enormous. In New York tourism is a massive business with holidaymakers often spoilt for choice. The city has progressed considerably from its humble beginnings when in the year 1000 Alconquin Indian Tribes used Manhattan for hunting and fishing.

Yes, to see New York, particularly that first time, takes some believing and this is the city that I visited to participate in its yearly marathon, because in November 2000 my wife and I visited New York for a few days holiday and were overwhelmed by the Big Apple. Whilst there I did occasionally think what it would be like competing in the city marathon. It had become quite an ambition of mine ever since I'd done the Boston Marathon in America four years previously. I'd been told by fellow marathoners that the New York Marathon was the best and an unforgettable experience so the seed was set and hopefully one day I would have the opportunity to do it. The sheer fascination of doing a marathon under those gigantic skyscrapers appealed to me immensely but it always seemed a dream which I thought would never materialise. But amazingly it did happen. I answered an advertisement in June 2001 in the London Marathon magazine which was asking anyone interested in the New York City Marathon to apply, the only stipulation being that a certain amount of the money raised would go to a certain charity. I therefore applied and was accepted. I was on my way and I could hardly contain myself with such undoubted pleasure and excitement and November 4th 2001 couldn't come quick enough for me.

The training started immediately for this marathon and having only completed the London Marathon in April of 2001, I knew I was in reasonable condition. It didn't particularly bother me that I would be competing in two marathons in a year. I felt it was quite within my capabilities and wild horses wouldn't stop me from doing it. I have to say that being a walker, which is how I do a marathon, takes me much longer than a runner would do it. Consequently, I am walking considerably more hours than a runner would be so with the endless hours of walking every day in my training programme , which was usually a good eight miles and increasingly more so as the date of November 4th drew closer. I was extremely busy because also most evenings I was out knocking on doors in the area where I live asking people to sponsor me. Therefore, with all the walking I was doing and the knocking on doors, it really was time-consuming and I had time for little else. I would like to compliment my wife here because in the year 2001 it wasn't easy for her and she has always been most supportive of all my sponsorship walking, but in the year 2001 with all the additional training, etc, she thought that two marathons was too much in one year.

I've been involved in raising money through my sponsorship walking since 1989 so writing this book gives me the ideal opportunity of thanking so many people, particularly where I live for the continued number of times these so generous subjects of Market Deeping and surrounding areas have sponsored me, their generosity knows no bounds. I couldn't have raised a penny if it wasn't for them. Being an ex-insurance man and trained to chat people up on the doorstep, I suppose it was comparatively easy for me to knock on any door and speak to the occupant. During my later years of working for the Prudential, many of my clients willingly sponsored me, whatever the cause I was raising money for. Strong friendships were formed with my customers which still exist today, even though I've been retired eight years I still go back and ask them to sponsor me for my yearly marathon, irrespective of the charity I've picked.

The charity I chose to compete in the New York City Marathon was "Get Kids Going". To create interest in what I was involved in, I circulated a letter to numerous clubs like Rotary, Lions, Women's Institutes and Mothers Unions, etc. and to many companies that operate in the area where I live. I therefore list the actual letter I sent to hopefully interested parties which I thought might sponsor me. This letter is self-explanatory and portrays how fortunate I've been in my lifetime to have played so many sports, not that I think I was anything special or even above the ordinary, because I wasn't, but most importantly I played sports because I was usually in good physical condition and not handicapped in any way. Others in this world are not so lucky.

THE NEW YORK CITY MARATHON 2001 –
WALKING FOR KIDS WHO CAN'T!
Sunday 4th November 2001

What would my life have been without sport. As I've

played at least a dozen sports in my lifetime, I cannot possibly imagine a life without sport. With my sporting life I've experienced good days and bad days and indifferent days and as I approach the later stages of my life, I'm still involved in sport, even though I'm reduced to such gentle pursuits as bowls and snooker but by far my favourite sport is walking. Yes, the very simple pleasure of walking which comes so naturally to me that I've always taken it for granted. But say the unthinkable had happened and all my life I'd been confined to a wheelchair.

"Get Kids Going" is a national charity which gives disabled children and young people up to the age of 26 years, the wonderful opportunity of participating in sport. It provides them with specially built sports wheelchairs, so they can do marathons, triathlons, tennis, athletics, basketball etc. It also provides personalised manual wheelchairs and trikes to use every day, at home, at school and to enable them to play with their friends.

On the 4th November, I shall be competing in the New York City Marathon. Being a walker I am hoping that my legs will carry me through this most exciting of all marathons, but some children in Great Britain who have no use in their legs will never experience the highs and lows I shall experience because they are disabled and have been confined to a wheelchair all their lives.

Please give me a donation so that I can help the "Get Kids Going" charity. Through sponsorship of me in this marathon, I hope to raise £3,000 towards the cost of a wheelchair. You see I was born lucky because I have great legs.

* * * * * *

The response to my letter was encouraging but I've always known that for me by far the best way to raise money for whatever the cause was talking to people on their own doorsteps. But would friends and ex-clients sponsor me twice in one year for this additional marathon? I obviously didn't want to rock the boat, asking those good people to sponsor me twice was taking advantage of them and the last thing I wanted to do was to upset anyone. But I need not have worried because the response was fantastic with over two hundred and fifty people sponsoring me, and if I was successful with the completion of the marathon the "Get Kids Going" charity would get their wheelchair. If I failed, they would get nothing. This is the way it's always been in my marathons. If I had failed to complete the marathon, all money collected would be returned to those who sponsored me. This way was always an added incentive for me to complete any marathon so the onus was definitely on me. I just had to complete the New York City Marathon.

I've never been so affected in such a way as I was when I heard of the horrendous occurrence which happened in New York on September 11th. I can think of other tragedies that have left me in a permanent state of shock - the 1957 Munich air crash in which many young Manchester United footballers were killed, the assassination of John F Kennedy, the President of the United States in 1963, John Lennon was brutally murdered in New York in 1980 and more recently the untimely death of Diana, Princess of Wales, in 1997 killed in a car crash in France. But nothing and I repeat nothing prepared me for the outrageous atrocity of September 11th. Everyone seems to remember where they were when terrible events happen and I can well remember where I was for the four tragedies mentioned and on September 11th I was speaking about India to a University of the Third Age Group in Louth, Lincolnshire. On arriving home and watching those dreadful TV pictures, it had the effect on me that the world had gone mad. The repeated pictures on TV of two hijacked airliners on suicide missions crashing into the twin towers of the World Trade Centre was quite unbelievable. Those pictures shook me to the core and it seemed so unreal as though I was watching a Hollywood film or a computer game. This wasn't for real I kept asking myself? As well as the twin towers being hit, another hijacked plane crashed into the Pentagon in Washington DC and a fourth airliner crashed into a field in Pennsylvania. Thousands of innocent people were slaughtered in an act of sheer wickedness that not only shook America but the whole of the world also. The world I fear will never be the same again.

The news had a devastating effect across America. Terrorism, apart from the Oklahoma bombing a few years previously, just did not exist in America and Americans had always felt reasonably safe. Whereas in my country, England, there was the constant threat of terrorism from the IRA. The British had lived with terrorism for years. America hadn't and wasn't ready for an attack that would stun the whole nation. George W Bush, who had been President for only a few short months having taken over from Bill Clinton, came on the country's TV network and promised that the perpetrators would be caught and brought to justice and told America to prepare for war. The sleeping giant had stirred and Americans wanted revenge. No way was a terrorist organisation going to be allowed to attack New York of all places and right in the very heart of Manhattan at that. America then went on full alert not only to prepare for further terrorist attacks but in preparation to hit back with weapons rarely seen since the Gulf War.

Within days Tony Blair, the British Prime Minister, had also declared that Great Britain was at war and stood shoulder to shoulder with America saying that terrorism must be defeated. In the aftermath of September 11th it must be said that only Great Britain had come to America's assistance and although the atrocity had been widely condemned by most nations on earth, very few expressed a willingness to be involved in defeating terrorism. It had been quickly established that Osama Bin Laden was the chief suspect having been involved with bombings in other areas of the world. Bin Laden's headquarters was in Afghanistan, a country ruled by the Islamic Fundamentalist Taliban. This cruel regime had occupied Afghanistan since the Russians had left the country in 1996 and were a ruthless oppressive regime which had outlawed all music and singing, friends couldn't even visit each others homes and even worse being that all children in the country would not attend schools as all education was banned, consequently women schoolteachers were not allowed to teach because women were not allowed to work and all women were forced to wear burkas which covered their faces, and all human rights taken from them. The Taliban ruled by fear where public executions and floggings were a regular occurrence. Afghanistan had always been a desperately poor country and under the Taliban it was a hundred times worse. This then was the country that allowed the notorious terrorist Osama Bin Laden and his Al-Qaeda organisation to plan their murderous attack on the World Trade Centre in New York on September 11th.

On first hearing about the events of this never to be forgotten day, my immediate thoughts were would the marathon still be allowed to take place which was just six weeks away? My great fear was that the authorities might call it off. Friends seemed to be forever informing me that I wouldn't be going. They seemed to think that it would be too big a risk for security reasons. The marathon would be the ideal opportunity for the terrorists to strike again, trying to protect not just the 25,000 athletes but the thousands of spectators on route would be impossible, I was being told, but I really would have been so disappointed if it had been cancelled. After all, this was the big one also the sponsorship money for the "Get Kids Going" charity had exceeded expectations. Purely, I think on the principle that little kids sitting in wheelchairs playing sports had created lots of sympathy, I had indeed touched a nerve with people who had been only too pleased to sponsor me.

So in the days leading up to the New York City Marathon nobody could question the American resolve, backed up to the hilt by Britain's Tony Blair with British troops preparing for war in Afghanistan. Meanwhile in Congress George W Bush gave the most effective performance of his short Presidency. "The hour is coming," warned the President and everyone knew that the United States of America was about to avenge the appalling loss of life suffered on September 11th. It was thought at this particular time roughly 5,000 people had been killed on September 11th at the World Trade Centre and the Pentagon in Washington DC. The President then stated he wanted Bin Laden dead or alive (shades of John Wayne here I thought) and it came as no surprise when on October 7th US and Britain launched air strikes on Afghanistan. The war had started as those devastating weapons were to be seen on our TV screens every night targeting Taliban strongholds. No one in his right mind wants war but by doing nothing Bin Laden would undoubtedly have struck again. Terrorism is evil and we had to attack those Taliban strongholds. The West hadn't started the war so there was no alternative. The innocent people I felt so dreadfully sorry for were Afghanistan's poor. They wouldn't even know what the war was all about, as if they didn't have enough problems with starvation on the ground and bombs raining down from the allies above. To be illiterate and poor, which millions are in Afghanistan at this time, must have been hell on earth.

The President had promised crushing retribution and on our TVs we were witnessing cataclysmic events in an increasingly dangerous world.

It was in the atmosphere of war, therefore, that I departed from England for New York on November 2nd. It was being reported in the media at this time that aircraft companies were losing a substantial amount of business with the cancellation of flights and some people did have a genuine fear of flying in view of what was happening in other parts of the world. I suppose there was the understandable fear that a British aircraft could be shot down as people were distinctly nervous because of Britain's involvement with America in Afghanistan. Sports stars and show-business people were openly refusing to fly in the conditions that prevailed. Sportsmen like the six Chelsea footballers who refused to fly to Israel to play for their Club. I suppose when one earns £45,000 a week like one of those footballers does, one can pick and choose whether one flies or not. Two of England's cricketers, Andrew Caddick and Robert Croft, after much discussion with their families and the bosses of cricket, refused to tour India last Winter because of the threat of terrorism. If only I was good enough and young enough I would have been the first on the plane and literally over the moon in the excitement of having been selected by my country to tour India to play cricket. The Daily Mail was most scathing of these sports stars and branded them cowards.

Tough guy Hollywood film stars also came in for severe criticism from the Mail. Bruce Willis of Die Hard films was referred to in the headlines as Willis the Wimp. The Mail said that Willis was nothing like as courageous as the character he portrays on the screen because he was too scared to fly to London for the premiere of his latest film. Muscle-man Arnold Schwarzenegger had also refused to fly to his homeland Austria to collect an

Honorary Doctorate citing September 11th. I felt that these well-known sports stars and show-business personalities should have set a better example. They are in the privileged position that they can refuse to fly. What about the thousands of British businessmen and salesmen and others who regularly fly off to various destinations of the world securing contracts for British workers at home. They fly to many of the world's dangerous areas and if they refused to fly they would undoubtedly be sacked. I have to admit I do not enjoy flying but nothing was going to stop me from competing in the New York Marathon and by my decision to fly at this particular time I did not think I was anymore brave than the next person because I believe that if one refuses to fly then the terrorists have won.

The flight to New York went well and the aircraft touched down at the John F Kennedy airport about 2 pm American time. On the plane were many athletes who would be competing in the marathon, with some even staying at the Wellington Hotel where I would be. After booking into the hotel on 5th Avenue some of us decided to register ourselves for the marathon at the City Expo Centre, which is something every athlete had to do in order to collect their race number. Without the race number there would be no marathon. So it was that with others I walked to 12th Avenue to get registered near the Joe D'Maggio highway and being out on those familiar and noisy streets and avenues again brought the memories of my previous visit flooding back. With Christmas not too far away it meant that I was in the very special atmosphere of the Big Apple again with shoppers galore on those glittering pavements. Those towering skyscrapers looked even higher as one strained one's neck on looking upwards to the sky. Yes, I was in New York and it felt great to be there again.

The walk to the Expo Centre and back was probably

about four miles and I know that walking around any city can be tiring, with New York being no exception. But on arriving back at the Wellington Hotel the walk had left me feeling absolutely shattered with my feet and legs aching intensely. I couldn't understand how this could be, particularly in view of the walking I'd done in training for this marathon. This worried me considerably with the marathon being staged the day after tomorrow. What hadn't helped was that it was a boiling hot day. I hadn't bargained for this heat because it was the Autumn of the year in New York. I do believe though that on rushing out of the hotel and the brisk walk to the Expo Centre amongst those vast crowds had obviously taken its toll on me, not forgetting, of course, I'd only just flown in from England hours before. Also, I could have been suffering from jetlag. I would therefore have to slow down and rest my aching feet and legs I told myself. I had to be unconditionally right for Sunday, November 4th, and the last thing I wanted to do was to undo all the hours of preparation for this marathon which I'd done in England.

Also that day I ventured on my own into Macy's, this so-world renowned department store, and I still have to smile to myself that I enquired about the buying of a comb there. I'd actually lost my comb so all I wanted was the very simple commodity of a comb. Now Macy's being the department store for the rich and famous who fly to New York from various places in the world just to go shopping there, and at the flick of a pen or the raising of an eyebrow, literally thousands of dollars are spent there. Now an Englishman in New York to be of smart appearance must have a comb and on enquiring at the sales counters the sales assistants were eyeing me up in a most peculiar way. I'm fairly sure that if I'd have enquired about the buying of a thousand combs those shop assistants might just have shown a little more enthusiasm, but that day in Macy's I may well have been rubbing shoulders with the multi-millionaires of this world, and the buying of one comb didn't seem a top priority or to stimulate any eagerness from those sales assistants to serve me. I can still clearly remember the differing looks I was getting from those sales assistants to this day, looks of disbelief that someone such as I could walk into this most magnificent and famous department store and enquire about the purchase of one solitary comb. Needless to say, I never was able to buy a comb in Macy's.

When I applied for entry into the New York City Marathon it meant that I would be sharing a twin-bedroom at my hotel with someone I'd never met before. It was actually four days and four nights I would be in the City and it does make one think that the someone might be a person with whom you have nothing whatsoever in common or it could be you can't stand the sight of each other which would have been worse. I need not have worried because the other athlete was a Nick Wright from Bristol and we seemed to hit it off almost immediately. In conversation he told me he was a partner in a firm of accountants in Bristol, was married with two teenage daughters. He followed soccer and played a regular round of golf and we had even more in common because we discovered we were both raising money through sponsorship for the same "Get Kids Going" charity. I was most fortunate with sharing a room with Nick. Conversation between us was always relaxed, easy and interesting and because we spent so many hours together it was just as well.

In the evening many competitors who had flown in from Great Britain and others who had arrived earlier were invited to a reception at the Mayflower Hotel, organised by the "Get Kids Going" charity. Nick and I attended this reception where we met many other marathoners and Jane Emmerson, the race organiser for "Get Kids Going" whom I thought gave a good welcoming speech and thanked everyone present for doing the marathon for the charity. We were told of heartbreaking and quite distressing stories of children who would be spending all their lives in wheelchairs. Jane Emmerson had evidently never run a marathon in her life and to my surprise others present that evening hadn't either but they didn't seem nervous or perturbed in any way and were really looking forward to an exciting day, a day I'm sure they would never forget. What impressed me about this gathering was the tremendous enthusiasm being shown by all the competitors. It left me with the feeling that I was definitely doing the marathon for the right charity and quite proud I was too. Also, if the fervour and eagerness were maintained throughout the marathon I had few fears that those athletes present that evening would not complete the marathon.

On arriving in New York for this second visit in twelve months I did sense that it was a slightly different New York than my previous visit. The whole atmosphere in the city had changed somehow since September 11th. I knew and probably expected it to be not as before but there was no doubt the city had changed. I would go so far as to say the city was still in mourning with New Yorkers still in a state of shock and still in disbelief that their great city could have been the target of such evil terrorism. It soon became very clear that anyone from Great Britain was being warmly welcomed by all New Yorkers and as there were two thousand Brits competing in the marathon, the welcomes we were getting were very genuine indeed. This had come about because of Britain's involvement in the war in Afghanistan in defeating terrorism with its staunch ally America. This was most noticeable in shops, hotels and out on the streets that people were pleased to speak to the British and I very quickly came to the conclusion that Tony Blair is a hero to the American people, purely on the issue of Britain supporting America against terrorism. It must also be said that Members of Parliament gave their full backing to its Prime Minister and that the majority of the British people supported Parliament at this time. Yes, the Brits could do no wrong during my second visit to New York. America really did appreciate my country's support otherwise it would have been very much isolated in the world in defeating terrorism and it was also stated at this particular time that Tony Blair was the most popular Prime Minister of Great Britain to the American people since Winston Churchill.

The day before the marathon with my new found friend Nick was spent in a most casual and relaxed way just wandering around the area of 5th Avenue reading newspapers and watching TV in our bedroom with, of course, the marathon being uppermost in our thoughts. That evening we attended yet another party, this time a party in Central Park for the whole of the registered marathoners. There were literally thousands of athletes there with free beer and food with music and everyone generally enjoying themselves. I have to say, however, it was hardly the time for drinking vast amounts of beer because the emphasis was very much on the next day which was fast approaching. While in Central Park Nick and I spent sometime at the well lit up finish line area where work was still going on by workmen in preparation for the marathon, where our thoughts at that precise time would be on whether we would make it to the finish line the next day. My New York Marathon was only hours away and I could already feel the tension creeping in and added to that the excitement of the occasion. I also knew that what happened on September 11th would be very much a part of the marathon as if they were inexplicably linked together in some way. I just hoped though above all else I could get a good night's sleep. If I could, I would have no fears that I couldn't do it. My determination and enthusiasm would hopefully see me through an Autumn day in New York I'm never likely to forget.

Chapter Two

The Marathon
(Keep Going Buddy)

On the day of the marathon I'm out of bed by 5 am. The reason for being up at such an unearthly hour was that there was a bus to catch which would be one of the official buses laid on especially for the occasion – The 2001 New York City Marathon. Buses were to be caught outside the City Library on Fifth Avenue between 5.30 am and 7.30 am, which would then transport me and thousands of other competitors to Staten Island where the start of the marathon was to be. As Nick was first into the bathroom, I sat on my bed to contemplate the day ahead. I must admit I was not enthralled with enthusiasm and if there was one marathon I wanted to be absolutely right for the task ahead, then this would be the one. Alas, I felt tired and jaded because I'd had another dreadful night's sleep. New York's traffic, so noisy throughout the night, was causing me some anxiety. I'd hardly had a wink of sleep during my two nights in the city but it was not to be and even my sleeping pills had little effect on me.

Would I complete the marathon was a question I repeatedly asked myself as I sat on that bed. If I had been fortunate enough to have slept well I would have felt quietly confident of completing this world famous marathon – but if I was tired before the start of a marathon and when I was obviously not in the right frame of mind, then what chance had I got? Had I not trained as hard for this marathon as any previous marathons? The hours and hours over endless months when I was to be seen walking every day on the streets where I live. Surely it would reward me handsomely or was it going to be a waste of time and effort?

But I quickly came to the conclusion that when an athlete ventures abroad, he must take into account that jetlag and a substantial loss of sleep, all add up to a feeling of fatigue. I couldn't understand though that when I completed the Boston Marathon in Massachusetts in 1997 I had coped reasonably well. What an idiot I would feel having travelled from Market Deeping to America and I failed to complete the race. The disappointment would be intolerable and so unbearable even to think about. But whatever my problems I had to try to stay positive otherwise what was the point? To be negative was not an option. After a wash and shave I did feel somewhat better and I didn't mention to Nick how I felt. Surely he had problems of his own like completing the marathon. Having changed into our race gear we put on our tracksuits to keep warm because the start time was at 11.50 am which was hours away.

The weather forecast for the day was to be cooler than previous days. The last thing I wanted was sweltering heat, which would only add to my troubles. I deliberately put my trainers in the bag I was carrying and settled for my comfortable shoes for going on the bus to Staten Island. I had been unhappy with my trainers from when I had first bought them a month earlier. One should never wear a new pair of trainers which one is uncomfortable with and they should be worn gradually to break them in first. It is far better to wear well-worn trainers which one is comfortable with but these new trainers still had a certain tightness around the toes. This was a worry because if my feet were a problem, I was in serious trouble. However, it was too late on the morning of the most important marathon of my life to do anything about it. I should have bought a new pair of trainers much earlier than I did. I could have kicked myself for being so stupid. As I left the hotel to catch one of those buses with Nick, I began to think whether my problems were escalating or were they being blown up out of all proportion? Either way my concerns wouldn't go away. To say I was worried was putting it mildly.

Once out of the Wellington Hotel there seemed to be athletes everywhere in droves making for the buses. On finally finding the end of the queue at Bryant Park, it was then a slow process to the front of the queue. I was thinking at this particular time that the way I was feeling I could have done without this hassle and by the time I got on the bus, I must have walked a mile. Surely, I thought, I've got enough walking to do without any additional walks. Goodness knows how many buses were required for transportation as literally thousands of athletes were there. The word buses is frequently used in America, whereas in Great Britain, of course, they would be referred to as coaches.

Once on the bus I could feel the tension building up. I wouldn't be the only one thinking of the day ahead. Nerves can get to anyone and I was surprised with myself that I was feeling quite nervous. I should have thought that I would have conquered this feeling in view of the amount of marathons I've done but I do know that suffering with nerves is not necessarily a bad thing before the start of a marathon. A lack of nerves can make an athlete over confident and that would never do. Nothing is sure in this world and should never be taken for granted. Yes I was definitely nervous but in my case I was nervous coupled with apprehension as to whether I could complete this marathon in view of how I felt. On sitting next to Nick on the bus I thought about his true feelings because this was his first ever marathon and he had travelled all the way to New York to compete in it. I had to admire him. He was also a season ticket holder at Bristol Rovers Football Club and never missed a home match. I told him jokingly that I wouldn't hold it against him that Peterborough United was in a higher division than Rovers.

After about forty-five minutes on the bus, followed by a fleet of other buses all carrying athletes, we then crossed over the quite majestic and striking looking Verrazano Narrows Bridge. The bridge is the link between Brooklyn and Staten Island which is separated by a stretch of water called The Narrows. Once on the Island and to the left of the bridge is the Hudson River and to the right of the bridge is the East River. Both rivers then curl either side of Manhattan Island which is clearly seen from Staten Island. With its population of just under 400,000, Staten Island is often referred to as the forgotten borough of the five New York boroughs and is easily the most thinly populated of the boroughs. Early settlers here in 1661 were Dutch and French farmers and it was an important British base during the Revolutionary War. It is a refreshing contrast to the hurly-burly noise of Manhattan and with its tranquil lifestyle, residents here feel as though New York City is another world away.

The Verrazano Narrows Bridge was the starting point for all the athletes and it would soon be closed to the general traffic, as would all the other roads on the marathon route. I was gradually, I'm pleased to say, becoming increasingly aware of what lay ahead. Going over that bridge was exciting enough on the bus and the thought of walking over it only added to the excitement. I was definitely feeling better and up for the challenge. On getting off the bus on Staten Island, I was immediately made aware of the security involved. Helicopters hovering above in the vicinity of the bridge and boats on the river below, all prepared for any act of terrorism. Police and security guards were in abundance and certainly making their presence felt. A large plot of wasteland at the end of the bridge had been put aside for these thousands of athletes to prepare for the race. On joining the queue for the starting area, which is surrounded by a high-wire fence which is obviously there to keep out ineligible entrants, I'm told by the race officials that I will not be allowed into the starting area until I have the appropriate marathon gear on which, of course, includes my trainers being worn and also my chip which records an athletes' time on completion of the marathon. Security is so tight and any baggage scrupulously searched.

The chip which is laced in an athlete's boot is what the wonderful world of technology is all about. It works in such a way that when the runner or walker passes the start line, the chip automatically starts to operate. Then when the athlete finally passes the finish line at the end of the race, the chip switches off. This gives the race officials the correct length of time it takes an athlete to complete a marathon. At the finish line the chip is then removed and kept by the officials. I feel the system works brilliantly as there can never be any dispute concerning the correct time as every second is recorded by the chip. The chip, incidentally, is only about $3/4$" in diameter, is made of plastic and is hardly noticed on the athlete's trainers

I got talking to a lady official who was in charge of the baggage drop-off area. What happens here is that when the athletes finally take off their tracksuits and any other personal belongings, these items are then put in their own baggage bag which is then given to the baggage officials. That bag, along with thousands of other bags, is then transported by lorries to Central Park where the marathon finishes and where the athletes pick up their bags later in the day. This is what the lady official said to me: "I'm proud of being here today in view of what happened on September 11th. I lost friends in the Twin Towers that day and some came from Staten Island. I help out here for every marathon but this year it is especially important that the marathon goes ahead. Also it's wonderful that people like yourself and others from around the world are here and we must carry on as normal. If this marathon had been cancelled the terrorists would have won".

"Jesus loves you," said the preacher in the Religious Tent. This tent had been put aside for any runner who wished to attend a service prior to the start of the marathon. There might have been two hundred athletes there as not one but four preachers spoke concerning the marathon. All of the four, I believe, were competing in the marathon. Nick and I took communion in this tent and again the terrible events of September 11th were mentioned. Some of the runners who were in that tent were running for loved ones lost. Always remember said one of the priests that whatever pain or discomfort you may experience during the race that "Jesus loves you and is always with you". Little did I realise then that later that day I would be hoping for divine intervention to help me through this toughest of all marathons.

During the course of a marathon and before, it is so important that athletes fight dehydration. The average runner will burn around 2800 calories of energy and lose over 5lbs of fluid during the course of a marathon. It is important, therefore, that athletes consume plenty of fluids otherwise fatigue can set in and make an impact on performance levels. So on the wasteland on Staten Island, thousands of athletes were to be seen forever drinking. Because of this excess amount of fluids being drunk, runners are then to be seen relieving themselves alongside the high-wire fence and bushes in their hundreds. This is most noticeable at all marathons. I'm sure people who have never been involved in marathons might find the whole thing repugnant or disgusting or even laughable. Also on this temporary site there are 550 portable toilets.

There were long lines of queues operating outside these toilets with male and female using the same toilet. The smell coming from those loos was most unpleasant. But, as always, every athlete seems to accept this as normal practice before the start of any marathon. The sniffing of foul air would be the last thing the athletes would be bothered with. I can assure you they would have far more important things to worry about. My big fear at this stage of the marathon day with nervous tension gaining eminence, was that I might well develop the trots (diarrhoea) myself. I felt weak enough as it was without having to sit on a toilet seat and then perhaps feel even weaker still.

Excitement was mounting as the start time of the race 11.50 am approached and at 11.20 am all competitors were informed to find their rightful positions in the race. By this time I'd wished Nick all the best and I would hopefully meet up with him later. We had talked about meeting in Rosie O'Grady's Pub after the race, which was also on 5th Avenue and not far from our Hotel. It was also to be the meeting place for all the 400 "Get Kids Going" competitors in the marathon where that evening I'm sure we would all have one hell of a thirst on, but that depended entirely on how I felt after the marathon and whether I was successful or not. I could hardly celebrate if I had failed, could I? To accommodate thousands of entrants in the marathon a corral system is used, my number being 40,862 in the colour red which was pinned to the front of my vest. It meant, therefore, that runners with numbers in green and blue were in the front of the red numbers. Evidently this system is the only way to separate the elite athletes from walkers or slow runners. This is worked out from one's average time of completing a marathon in the last two years. Consequently 95% of all the competitors were lined up in front of me.

Now the tension was really building up with the start

drawing closer, although the disabled people in their wheelchair hand cycles had already started their marathon at 10.20 am. While waiting for the start and lined up with thousands of competitors, I got casually talking to a walker who had Brazil stamped across the front of his vest. I quickly realised that he wasn't fluent in English. Strange how sport can immediately break down barriers by having something in common. As he was from Brazil there was one word he simply must know I thought; and the word is the name of a famous soccer player who was born in Brazil in 1940, and it's widely regarded by everyone who saw him play that this man was the greatest soccer player the world has ever seen. "Pele" I said. His face lit up with the broadest smile. "Great man" he said. He then proceeded to further the conversation. "Great also yours he said. What's he talking about? He was pleading with me to understand him. "Your keeper, great save," he said. I instinctively knew what he was trying to tell me because Gordon Banks, the England goalkeeper in 1970 against Brazil in Mexico in the World Cup made a superlative save from a Pele header. "Greatest save I ever saw" said the Brazilian. I'm never likely to see that man again and we shook hands and wished each other well. The wonderful world of sport had briefly brought together two different nationalities from across the world for just a few minutes. What would the world be without sport?

Now to the most emotional and traumatic start to any marathon that I'm ever likely to be involved in – probably the most passionate ever. I believe many athletes that day would have considered themselves extremely fortunate to have just been there, even though that weekend America had been warned of another terrorist attack. But just ask those runners if they would sooner have been elsewhere, "No way" they would have said. This race had been put in jeopardy many times because of what happened on

September 11th. A spokesman for the marathon had said "that the status of the marathon was uncertain but now the race was here the marathon is symbolic of a people moving forward one step at a time. We think people see the marathon as helping". He was referring, of course, to the general reaction of New Yorkers who above all else wanted things to be as normal.

With just a few minutes to go to the voice of Mayor Rudy Giuliani booms over the microphone – this being the man who was so determined that the marathon would still be on - "Freedom is going to win, thousands of athletes and millions of New Yorkers are lining up united in their feeling that we are not afraid to exercise that freedom, United we run", he said. He then praised every one of the athletes for being there, especially those from abroad. As he spoke, 50 white doves were released. Britain had the largest contingent of athletes, 2000 of them represented among the 25,000 present. Evidently one hundred athletes were in attendance from different nations around the world. I doubt if in the history of New York has there ever been a more popular Mayor than Rudy Giuliani. Cometh the hour, cometh the man, and this man responded quite magnificently to New York's time of need. He is an inspirational figure who just happened to be in the right place at the right time. America's National Anthem was then sung very passionately by the Americans present, followed by the band playing "God Bless America" with those very same Americans chanting U.S.A. U.S.A. U.S.A. The whole atmosphere really was electric. I could feel the hairs on the back of my neck standing up. Never have I been so moved and I'm sure I speak for thousands of athletes when I say I was deeply affected by the occasion. Who would not be? One would have to have a heart of stone not to be. I was choked with emotion and I felt tears in my eyes and I was equally sure that the millions of viewers watching on TV throughout America were also moved by the occasion. The sheer pride I felt standing on the Verrazano Narrows Bridge made me feel proud to be British and, being a patriot, I felt that I was representing my country. I couldn't have felt more proud standing on that bridge than if "God save the Queen" was being sung.

The reason I was affected in such a way was that I still could not comprehend the appalling atrocity that happened on that dreadful day. That evil and murderous day that stunned the world and here was I representing all that was good in the world and that terrorism must be defeated. This New York City Marathon which would have real significance because it had not surrendered to terrorism - and why should it? – the Race President and his officials were to be congratulated on the stance they took and were so very keen that the marathon should still proceed. "God Bless America" for having the courage not to cancel the marathon. The world required strong leadership from America and New York was so assuredly doing just that. After all the drama of such a unique occasion, I felt I was ready for anything this marathon could offer. I was now simply raring to go. All thoughts of fatigue were now completely put out of my mind and body. Rudy Giuliani's speech so magnificent in its delivery had the effect that I just knew that I would complete this marathon. I hadn't travelled thousands of miles from my home to fail. I would give it my absolute all. I would beat any pain barrier thrown at me and if it meant completing the race on my hands and knees, then so be it. (Little did I think that later on that day I would see one such person actually doing that). The Mayor's words had been like a drug to me and I was well and truly hooked. Hooked by the occasion. Never had I been so determined about anything in the whole of my life and when the Mayor finally lit the fuse for the massive gun cannon followed by a big bang, whose voice should also come over the microphone singing "New York, New York" but the one and only Frank Sinatra. How appropriate that was and what a send off. I then took my first step in the New York City Marathon, a marathon which will be instilled in my memory forever. The adrenaline was not just flowing but pumping like mad. This was to be the marathon of all marathons to be staged anywhere in the world and I was to be part of it and when I'm an old man I shall look back with affection on a marvellous occasion and proudly say I was there.

The Verrazano Narrows Bridge is about two miles long. A two-tier bridge, it is most impressive just to look at it. Not so impressive though is when one has to run or walk over it. This massive structure was built in 1964 and it became the world's longest suspension bridge. At its highest point it is 274 feet above sea level. It's easily the best form of travel for commuters going to work and shoppers travelling in their motor cars from the Island to Manhattan. I knew immediately that even though I was pumped up with enthusiasm, this particular marathon would cause me many problems. The steady uphill incline to the middle of the bridge had such an effect on me that at times I didn't think I'd make it. Because of this incline my leg muscles were really aching and my feet felt on fire. I quickly came to the conclusion that in the vicinity of my home in Market Deeping there's not a hill in sight. All my walking in the months leading up to the marathon had been done on extremely flat roads. Consequently, I was not used to walking up hills because I'd never tried any. Walking up this bridge, therefore, was something entirely new to me. "Crikey I'm not going to make it" were my thoughts. I was also sweating profoundly and the weather forecast was wrong. Cooler weather for the day had been forecast which is the way I like it. It was a lovely day though and I would just have to grin and bear it. One of the reasons I like competing in marathons and the stimulation it gives me is the challenge of the race itself, and this huge bridge was certainly giving me a hell of a challenge of some proportion.

The bridge was packed to capacity on both tiers with thousands of athletes at last on the move. Being on the top tier I was quite amazed that already within a few minutes of the race starting, runners could be seen once again relieving themselves. There were literally scores of them lined up on the side of the bridge letting nature take its cause. The problem for the runners underneath in the first tier, however, would be that they were being watered on from a great height. With my warped sense of humour I had to smile to myself because the runners below must have been getting a thorough soaking on the most beautiful day imaginable without a cloud in the sky. At the start of any marathon and probably for a good quarter of an hour there is always a lot of shoving, bumping and juggling for positions by the athletes. This happens because of the sheer number of athletes in the race. Obviously with the competitors so keen to get moving, sometimes rough treatment is handed out. Walkers like myself are continually being knocked about from runners overtaking. Eventually, though, the walkers at the rear of any marathon are well left alone. Because all the runners are then in front of him, he can then plan his marathon according to what time he hopes to complete the race by. He is at last in control of his own destiny. This is the way I like it, completely on my own and well away from other athletes. I know then that I can quite easily walk the first four miles in under the hour.

On nearing the half way point of the bridge and on going up and up and up, I looked to the left and saw the spectacular view of the Lower Manhattan skyline about five miles away in the distance. But, alas, the World Trade

Centre was missing and the Twin Towers were no more and I knew that the New York skyline would never be the same again. How could it possibly be? So, it was as though there was a large, empty space – or should I say a big hole – in the middle of those tremendously high buildings. Those skyscrapers were actually dwarfed by the Twin Towers so massively high they were and, of course, they were the highest buildings in New York. I particularly remember that skyline from when I first saw it because my wife and I had visited the Statue of Liberty Island a year previously. This Island in New York Harbour sits between Manhattan and New Jersey, the first look of America for the thousands of immigrants from across the world would be the Statue of Liberty. Surely a most welcoming sight. The Statue of Liberty was made in France and unveiled in New York Harbour in 1886 and it was from Liberty Island that my wife and I had stood for some considerable time as we gazed in awe at the incredible sight of Manhattan, so extraordinary that it took one's breath away.

I suppose if Osama Bin Laden was planning another terrorist attack on New York, the Verrazano Narrows Bridge was a prime target and as good a place as any to strike, considering the amount of athletes on it then. It was an obvious target. Thousands, not just hundreds, could have been killed and amongst unprecedented security the like of which none of those athletes had seen before. All the competitors were on the move. "United we Run" had been the slogan of the race and nothing would deter those athletes. Armed guardsmen and even sniffer dogs were to be used on all the five City bridges. Divers had even checked the supports of the bridges crossed. Certainly in the history of marathons worldwide there had never been such tight security and I must admit I did feel a slight sense of relief when I finally crossed that bridge. If there was to be another attack on New York that day, at least America would be ever alert and ready to respond quickly and decisively against any terrorist attack. Lessons had been cruelly learned and Bin Laden had so dramatically caught America cold. Hopefully it will never happen again.

Once over the bridge I was then in the Borough of Brooklyn. It was here that crowds of spectators had gathered. Thousands of people were waving flags (mostly the American flag I might add) and cheering and clapping. The crowds on those pavements were so ecstatic, their welcome was quite overwhelming and never in any of my previous marathons had I seen such crowds. Sometimes six deep on the pavements either side of the road. Their appreciation of any athlete was so blatantly obvious – "Keep Going Buddy" – was a constant reminder for me to stick with it. "Good Lord" I thought, if the crowds are as enormous and enthusiastic as this along the route, how could I possibly fail? How could I not make it to Central Park? The intensity of the crowds left me on a permanent high. These Americans with their wild encouragement must have lifted any lingering doubts I may have had as to whether I could complete this race. Literally thousands had come to cheer others and me on the New York City streets. With the singing of "God Bless America" still ringing in my ears, I was well and truly up for the challenge. Having recovered and over the first hurdle of that bridge I had settled into a nice walking rhythm. With my legs and arms moving as they should, I felt in good condition and nicely relaxed. Above all else, I wanted to enjoy the marathon and I could only do that providing my body was sending out the correct signals.

On my vest is printed in large letters "Get Kids Going", this being, of course, the charity I was competing for in the marathon. Many times the crowds on seeing me would shout "Come on Get Kids Going" or "Good luck Get Kids Going". But by far the most popular was "Keep Going

Buddy". Never have I been called Buddy so much in all my life, although I do recall being called by that very same name in the Boston Marathon. If New Yorkers do not know your name, it is most convenient for them to address you as Buddy. Even in ordinary conversation, whether out shopping or speaking to someone on the City streets and definitely in a pub they will refer to you as Buddy. Also on the front of my vest is printed "Number One Team". This is because "Get Kids Going" had more athletes from Great Britain than any other British Charity competing in the race. So those vast crowds had even spotted that and sometimes they would shout "Keep Going Buddy, Number One Team".

Because of the horrific events on September 11th, several entrants who had qualified for this marathon had perished in the Twin Towers. However, the race authorities had made exceptions and husbands, wives, sons, daughters and other close relatives had been allowed to take the places of their loved ones. How I admired those people because maybe some of them were not even runners or walkers anyway, so it would be doubly difficult for them. Also, they may well have been even more affected than the other athletes by the sheer emotion of this marathon. Maybe also they had tears in their eyes as they strove to make it to Central Park. These people's attitude put this marathon in its proper perspective because whatever worries I may have had as regards completing this race, I quickly realised that my troubles or fears were simply nothing in comparison. I hadn't lost a wife. I hadn't lost a son or daughter. How would I have coped with that? These are often life's unanswered questions but these stand-in runners do have my deepest admiration.

Among these enthusiastic and passionate crowds, I saw many placards being held aloft. As I couldn't quite understand what message those placards were giving, I deliberately edged my way closer to the side of the road to try to understand what was written on them. One such lady held her placard with a large photograph of someone in her family who had been lost in the Twin Towers, with the words in large letters saying "Thanks for doing it for him". Lots of other placards gave similar messages. Those spectators were so pleased that the marathon hadn't been called off because, as I've previously written in this book, this marathon could have been called off at any time over the previous two months. Those placards with their poignant messages would also be an added incentive to all the competitors to complete the race. The messages would also be for athletes who were in the race to raise money through sponsorship for a fund founded by Mayor Rudy Giuliani for the relatives of dear ones lost on September 11th.

After about five miles of being on 4th Avenue, I saw a name which will forever be familiar to me. There it was, the name Prudential above one of the many shops on what would normally be a very busy shopping road. Because of that name I immediately felt at home, the reason being that I'd been employed by The Prudential for 29$^1/_2$ years until I was made redundant in 1993. Prudential is a very big name indeed in America and the name is to be seen everywhere. The pride I felt on working for The Pru was immense and even in retirement the pride is still there today. When I completed the Boston Marathon in 1997, right opposite the finish was the name Prudential which was lit up on top of one of the City's highest buildings shining down on me. I'll never forget that. There is even a tube station in Boston called Prudential. The Pru pays my pension – long may its prosperity continue.

I must be getting old I thought because after about seven miles and still on 4th Avenue I was beginning to show signs that all was not well. My hobbling had started early and as I have arthritis in my right ankle, this was nothing new and I firmly believe that all the walking I do I am at least fighting it. I know my ankle will never be as it was once and my Doctor has told me several times that I will eventually have to stop this excessive pressure I am putting on it, but I refuse to stop walking. Maybe I am obstinate or silly and downright stupid, but I really do love walking and the pleasure I get from it is immeasurable. Because of my love of cricket, having played the game to the age of 58, I honestly didn't think anything in sport could possibly or even remotely replace cricket, but on having discovered the joys of walking it gives me now nearly as much pleasure as cricket ever did. But the reason I say that I must be getting old was not necessarily because I was limping, but that I'd suffered the indignity of being overtaken by an elderly gentleman who was many years older than me. If my self-esteem was damaged, there was simply nothing I could do about it. I wouldn't say it was humiliation but it was close. I might add that I am no Spring chicken myself these days but I do feel for my age I keep in reasonable shape. This walker, however, who so casually overtook me was twenty-five years older than me. I couldn't believe it.

I had met this elderly gentleman at the 2001 London Marathon on 18 April last year. I had got used to seeing his back because I had trailed behind him for many miles and when I eventually caught up with him, we had both completed twenty-two miles. I formed a conversation with him as we walked together for part of the last four miles. It helps to pass the time away and if one can concentrate on anything but that day's marathon, then that must be a good thing. Anything to relieve extreme tiredness and an aching body. On talking to him he told me he was from New York. I then asked him a very impertinent question hoping, of course, that I wouldn't offend or be rude to him in anyway. "I hope you won't mind me asking you, but how old are you," I said. "I'm ninety-one" he replied. I was dumbstruck by his answer. It seemed hardly credible that such an elderly person who had reached such an age and was still competing in marathons around the world, what an inspiration he must be for any of us as we go into old age? Was it mind over body for him that he can convince himself he is not yet ready for the carpet slippers? It was my privilege to have spoken to him and my admiration for him grew because of our conversation and here he was overtaking me in this New York City Marathon. Admittedly he had two teenage girls either side of him, probably in case any harm came to him like falling over. I would love to have spoken to him again but he was soon lost on the horizon. No consolation for me was that he may have had a birthday since I last saw him, making him 92 years of age. His name was Abraham Weintraub.

New York traffic cops are such gentle souls and I'm positively sure they have never been called that before. The whole wonderful atmosphere of the race was helped by so many obliging police officers. I heard that there were over 3,000 of them on the marathon route. If that were true, then there were over 3,000 smiling faces. Even they were encouraging me with the immortal words of "Keep Going Buddy". But those vast crowds that were so enthusiastic before were rapidly diminishing fast. This happens at all marathons because people will only watch a marathon for so long and consequently when the walkers appear many hours later, some of the streets are nearly deserted. But it is the walkers who probably need even more encouragement than the leaders in a marathon. Many of the runners, certainly the winner, will have run the 26 miles in just over two hours. Thousands of runners will run it in under three hours and thousands more in under four hours and so on. But the walkers, of course, take considerably longer. So just imagine how the walker feels when he's completed his 26 miles. He is definitely on his feet many hours longer than the runners but the Brooklyn cops who had such a large part to play in this marathon were so considerate and patient with the walkers, particularly as the side streets were trying to get back to some form of normality. Those superb traffic police officers were quite wonderful towards the walkers, often holding up the traffic so walkers like myself could proceed on their way.

After about $8^{1}/_{2}$ miles, having finally left 4th Avenue, I proceeded up Lafayette Avenue. I say up because that is precisely what it was. The slight incline up was nothing I'm pleased to say in comparison to the Verrazano Narrows Bridge. But if ever I wanted a lift then this was it because every so often on a marathon, whether one is a runner or walker, any sort of help is appreciated. At this stage of the race I received what was without question one of the highlights of the entire marathon. Now whether it was because I was limping and the spectators were giving me sympathy I'll never know, but walking along Lafayette Avenue my leg muscles were pulling again and my feet really were beginning to give me problems. This I fear had come about by the tightness of my toes in my trainers and just when I thought most of the crowds had gone home, I came across a group of spectators who greeted me with thunderous applause. It undoubtedly acted as a tonic to me and just when I needed it. I suppose I could have been highly embarrassed by the reception they gave me. After all, who was I to be so deserving of such a welcome of such magnitude?

Half way along this avenue, I approached a very large group of spectators. They had moved off the pavements and there they were forming a human column of people for me to walk through right in the centre of the road. Never in my life have I ever experienced such a momentous amount of cheering, clapping, whistling and backslapping. As the nearest walker was a good two hundred yards in front of me and the same behind me, I was completely on my own. There must have been three hundred people in this human column and as I approached them the noise they made was quite deafening. "Thanks for coming Buddy" was continually shouted at me. Their tumultuous greeting took my breath away, particularly when I had to keep coming up for air from this continuous back slapping. I could do no wrong. Having taken off my cap I was clapping them with my hands above my head in appreciation of their glorious reception to me. This went on for quite a few minutes. How could I possibly repay these Americans for their welcome? At that precise moment one of the ways of thanking them would be for me to complete this marathon. The effect they had on me was quite amazing. I felt ten feet tall and all that confidence I had previously came bouncing back and I carried on with increased energy and I was so appreciative of such wonderful support.

When one walks through any area for the very first time, one is most interested in the surroundings and on walking through Brooklyn I really did have a panorama view of all around me. I saw many shops and supermarkets with flats above and occasionally churches, just like any areas in Great Britain. I was surprised to see that many of the detached houses are made of wood and most impressive they are but it did cross my mind how these wooden houses could stand up to the demands of New York Winters where they do have considerably more snow than my country. Because of a huge influx of immigrants spread over many years, much of Brooklyn's stylish neighbourhoods are now slums and this does create a breeding for crime. Brooklyn's huge population is a mixture. There is a large Jewish community and thousands of African-Americans have settled there. There are also many immigrants from the West Indies. Generally though all immigrants have settled in well but it is certainly a colourful mixture of different nationalities. There are also the most beautiful residential areas where famous Brooklynites Barbara Streisand and Woody Allen have homes in the area making Brooklyn in parts very wealthy indeed. From what I've seen of Brooklyn it has many advantages and seems to be a popular place to live. Incidentally, 2 to $2^{1}/_{2}$ million people live there.

There is a large Jewish community in Brooklyn which I was made very aware of as I walked along Bedford Avenue, all at once it seemed that the white and coloured children who had been so evident before, were replaced by Jewish children all wearing their yarmulke caps, who were frequently following me and in a most inquisitive way were asking me all sorts of questions, and for some reason had big smiles on their faces when I told them I was from England. Brooklyn's Williamsburgh district has long been an area for the Satmer Sect which originated from Hungary, most noticeable were the male Jews in their dark frock coats with beards and side curly dreadlocks hanging down under big broad brimmed black hats. The heads of Jewish women had their heads covered having had their heads shaved. All the sect's schools and synagogues are in this neighbourhood. I thoroughly enjoyed walking through this very ultra strict Satmar Sect. The males all dressed completely in black were most pleasant and sociable to me and the so well behaved children quite delightful. It was an education for me walking through that part of Brooklyn, an area of New York which I shall not easily forget.

Marathons are often full of surprises and sometimes I am worryingly surprised by the non-fitness of some of these competitors who might well be trying a marathon for the very first time. Just occasionally, I've come across a competitor who might be grossly overweight and generally unfit to do a marathon, not that I think a person who is overweight shouldn't try a marathon because that is entirely up to him or her, but I seriously believe that these people just do not know what they are letting themselves in for because if they are not fit and haven't trained properly, then they have little chance of succeeding because they are well and truly found out. On regularly seeing these first-time marathon entrants, I feel they are putting a tremendous strain on their heart and it has also been known for athletes to have heart attacks while doing a marathon. On always being at the rear of marathons, I regularly come into contact with them. They start well enough but often fail to complete five miles and are then picked up by the marathon sweep bus which trails behind all the walkers. On seeing these people and often talking to them with words of encouragement, I am naturally concerned for their health. Incidentally, sweep buses are always at the rear of all marathons. These buses will pick up any runner or walker who is injured or experiencing gross fatigue and simply cannot partake in the marathon any more.

Having written that, I can think of one such walker in this marathon where I have to admit I got it horribly wrong and one should not judge anyone by appearances only. I had followed this walker for about a mile and he seemed in such bad condition he looked on the point of dropping out. Several times he was swaying considerably as if he might be falling over and he was one of those people who looked overweight and I actually thought he shouldn't be in this marathon. He should do the sensible thing and not go any further. He should catch the sweep bus, I thought, he really was in a poor way and obviously a person who was doing his first marathon. Or so I thought. As I drew level with him before overtaking, I had a good look at this first-time marathon walker. He looked about forty-five years of age and if looks are anything to go by, he looked terrible. He was perspiring so much that it looked as if he had had a bucket of water thrown over him. He was absolutely saturated. My words of conversation with him and his replies went something like this.

"How are you?" I ask.

"Fine Buddy" he grunts the reply.

"I suppose this is your first marathon then" I ask him in quite a chirpy way.

"No Buddy" he replies. I admit to being surprised by this answer.

"How many marathons have you done then?" I ask.

"Nineteen" he quickly replies. I was rather taken back by this reply and out of curiosity I continued to question him.

"Not nineteen?" I ask slightly raising my voice.

"Yes nineteen" he growls an irritable reply. This conversation was getting more interesting by the second or it was going nowhere fast, I thought.

"I meant New York marathons" I ask him.

"Yes, nineteen" as he raises his voice in reply and I begin to think that the American is getting slightly cheesed off with this inquisitive Englishman who keeps on asking such impertinent questions.

"Listen Buddy, this is my nineteenth consecutive New York Marathon" he replies in a rather loud pitched voice.

"Wow, not nineteen consecutive New York Marathons" I reply in rather an excitable way, which I did think was an incredible achievement.

He then mutters something which I fail to understand. It may well have been strong language and I smile to myself what he could be saying and I finally get the message that the American is running out of patience with me. No doubt I was sapping his energy but I would love to know what his final answer was which he muttered under his breath. Now if the reader of this book has a sense of humour, just think what that guy's last words might have been to me. I can think of a couple of beauties, which I shan't mention here.

I continued on my way happy in the knowledge that I'd tried to help someone in this marathon by forming a conversation. Whether my American friend was as happy I'm not so sure. Maybe he felt even worse for briefly meeting me. Most noticeable in this marathon was that there was not the usual fancy dress outfits being worn like there is in the London Marathon. There were some, of course, but nothing in comparison to the London Marathon where a good 15% of all the competitors are dressed in some of the strangest outfits imaginable making the London Marathon an extremely colourful occasion where charity runners and walkers in their thousands raise money for different charities, where men dressed as women wearing wigs, make-up, large breasts and even larger breasts, with suspenders and mini-skirts and carrying buckets through the crowds of onlookers on the pavements and hoping to find people in a generous mood. At the time of writing it has just been announced that on the last London Marathon on April 18th 2001, £24 million pounds has been raised for charities. What a staggering amount that is but just because the Americans are not to be seen in fancy dress outfits, it doesn't mean that less money will be raised than the London Marathon because I know that in all probability this New York city Marathon will raise millions of dollars in view of the atrocity on September 11th which will undoubtedly make it the biggest money raising marathon of all time.

Some of the competitors in marathons have done some of the most unusual things possible. Once in a London Marathon I saw a man walking backwards for the whole of the 26 miles. He told me that the money he was raising by people sponsoring him to walk backwards was for cancer relief. Goodness knows how long it took him to complete the race. Maybe he finished it the next day because on talking to him as I overtook him he was really struggling. Just think about walking backwards for one mile, let alone 26 miles. Yes, I've seen some incredible things done in marathons by people raising money for charities but nothing compares to what I saw in the New York City Marathon and it was about the 11th mile that I came across one such young man who was doing the marathon on his hands and knees, all for the cause of charity. This young man was literally dragging himself along on his hands and knees and quite a large crowd of spectators were following him. I'm sure in total admiration for what he was doing. As I overtook him I glanced down at him to see how he could possibly keep going. Strapped to both legs from the knee to his ankle he was padded up with heavy padding which protected his legs from the hard surface of the road. On both knees and ankles he had small metal rollers which were fixed to the padding and in the kneeling position he was able to use his hands by putting one hand in front of the other and pull himself along the road on the rollers. Needless to say, he was wearing thick heavy gloves to also protect his hands from the roads' surfaces. I never read anything about this man in any of the New York newspapers afterwards. Maybe he didn't finish the marathon. Maybe he could still be out there on his tortuous journey.

After a good four hours and approaching the 12-mile point, I was sweating like a pig. The temperature seemed to be rising considerably and I was again having doubts as to whether I could complete this marathon. It was tough going and I cursed the weather forecasters for getting it wrong. In all honesty I hadn't bargained for the heat and it was sapping my energy and I felt really sluggish. I was also hitting the wall as all athletes will know about when the going gets tough. It's as though one is pushing one's body through an invisible wall as one battles to keep going. What was particularly galling was that when I was in New York just a year earlier, the temperature was the other way. It was bitterly cold and I had therefore taken this into account when I visited New York the second time, thinking of course how cold it would be and here I was twelve months later perspiring profusely. Also, tucked away at the back of my mind was the amount of sleep I'd lost since leaving England. Maybe it was beginning to have some effect. I knew at this stage of the marathon I would be desperately tired by the time I reached Central Park. What didn't help also was the state of the New York City roads which I have to report are notoriously bad with many potholes making it an unyielding surface for all competitors.

On thirteen miles I was on Berry Street and it was the halfway point. Now to keep the concentration and the momentum going it was time for me to sing, yes sing. Whether it is long walks or short walks I can sing merrily away to myself. There's plenty of wide, open spaces in the area of Lincolnshire where I live and, fortunately, nobody can hear me but I can think of a group of friends who might well cringe at the very thought. They have heard me sing at New Year's Eve parties and I'm sure if Frank Sinatra were alive today he would categorically state "He ain't no singer". But Sinatra happens to be a particular favourite of mine and the song I sung on this New York City Marathon has been made famous by old blue eyes himself. Sinatra was born at Hobokin, New Jersey, which is just across the Hudson River from Manhattan and he described this ballad as a perfect song. Apparently the lyrics and music were written by Vernon Duke and as I was in New York and visiting the city again and as it was also the Autumn of the year with the leaves gently falling off the trees, what could be more appropriate than for me to sing "Autumn in New

York". The words are poignant in view of what happened on September 11th.

"Autumn in New York
Why does it seem so inviting
Autumn in New York
It spells the thrill of first nighting
Shimmering clouds, glittering crowds
In canyons of steel
They're making me feel I'm home
Yes its Autumn in New York
That brings the promise of new love
Autumn in New York is often mingled with pain
Lovers with empty hands
All long for exotic lands
But Autumn in New York
It's good to live it again"

Lines ten and eleven are pitifully sad and in the Autumn of the anniversary date in New York the memory of that ghastly and cowardly day will never be forgotten. How can it possibly not be remembered when so many families throughout the world have been traumatized. New York in the Autumn will forever be mingled with pain and lovers will have empty hands from loved ones lost who on September 11th never returned home.

On saying goodbye to Brooklyn, I then crossed over the Pulmski Bridge, which links Brooklyn to Queens. The bridge, of course, is a major roadway in normal circumstances but I virtually had the bridge to myself and it's probably more of a flyover than a bridge and thousands of New York motorists would use this bridge every day going about their business. Looking down from a great height I could see a river which joins the East River and literally thousands of buildings which would comprise houses, flats, shops, department stores, schools and factories and probably a large dockland area as well. I must have looked a lone figure as I battled to walk up the bridge's incline. I think also that it must have been the hottest part of the day on that bridge and apart from my sore feet, I had settled down to a nice walking rhythm again. This rhythm is so important to a walker like myself and it also means I am walking well within myself. But I also knew at this stage of the marathon that my time would be my slowest for a marathon ever and I was still a long way from the finish. Never would I have been on my feet for so long. If determination was anything to go by and providing my enthusiasm and concentration were there, then I would do it but being a long distance marathon walker can be a very lonely business indeed and just occasionally to chat with a fellow walker is a bonus. Even an avid walker like myself can get lonesome and would welcome the company of another walker but on that bridge there was not an athlete in sight. "Where is everybody?" I thought.

At the very highest point of the Pulmski Bridge I was once again struck by the magnificence of the Manhattan skyline. I even considered myself extremely fortunate just to be there for free. Even without the Twin Towers I couldn't help myself by continually looking across to my left and seeing those towering skyscrapers across the East River. They really are an awesome sight and I was marvelling at its architecture and taking in the breathtaking views of the Big Apple. The sheer beauty of the Manhattan skyline reminded me of the Taj Mahal in the City of Agra in India, the similarity being that I was looking at one of the wonders of the world. The Taj Mahal is the miracle of miracles, the jewel in India's architectural diadem. The graceful white marble structure shines with awe-inspiring loveliness and I spent most of the day when I visited it just looking and walking around it. That's exactly how I felt on the Pulmski Bridge. I could have stayed for hours on that bridge taking in the general view of the whole of the New York skyline. But I couldn't stop for one single moment, otherwise my walking would have totally disintegrated and I would in all probability never have been able to start again. After all I was hardly on a sightseeing tour but I never thought that until I saw the Taj Mahal and the Manhattan skyline that something built by man could be so enchanting and pleasurable on the eye, but it is.

Once in the borough of Queens and at the end of the bridge there was a group of smiling Police Officers waiting to greet me with the inevitable "Keep going Buddy". They also assured me that I was still on the marathon route which was a relief because there was literally no one in sight. I was hardly likely to catch up with anyone either unless, of course, athletes in front of me were slowing down. There are supposed to be on all marathons Race Marshalls who should be seen every mile of the marathon route but, alas, I didn't always see them. With the directions from the police, however, I was now on Jackson Avenue. Queens is the largest of the five boroughs and is also technically on Long Island. About 2 million people reside there. It is not necessarily a quiet place to live either because of the John F Kennedy and La Guardia Airports and it does have endless rows of monotonous-looking terraced houses. But Queens fits the bungalow and two-garage image of a typical American family living in a big city. Just like Brooklyn, the community of Queens also reflects New York's immigration patterns and here there are huge areas very much dominated by Puerto Ricans and Greeks. I really was getting a remarkable observation to some extent of the inner city areas of New York and to a lesser extent the American way of life. This land of liberty, freedom and opportunity for all really has attracted citizens from all the nations on earth. What better way therefore was there for me to explore these five boroughs with open eyes while walking through them. I can categorically state that I've been to the very heart of one of the world's most exciting cities and sometimes I had to pinch myself that this was happening to me. Yet if somebody had said to me years ago that I would go to America and compete in two marathons there I just wouldn't believe them. Strange how one's life can turn out.

Now that I was in the Borough of Queens and drawing ever closer to it, even though it was just across the East River I couldn't help but notice one of New York's best loved buildings. Between those endless blocks of monotonous terraced houses it stood like a peacock proud of all it surveys. Yes, the enduring Empire State Building which is situated in midtown Manhattan. Opened in 1931, it has been undoubtedly one of the City's prime attractions. Due to a construction mania which swept through the city during the 1920's, the Empire State Building became the world's tallest, taking the title from the Chrysler Building which many think is more beautiful than the Empire State Building. In 1973, however, the World Trade Centre – the Twin Towers – were built and then became the highest building in New York. But with the Twin Towers no more, the Empire State Building is once again the tallest building in the city. The view from the very top is quite spectacular and for any visitor to New York it is an absolute must to see. With my wife, we visited the Empire State Building and its scenery from the top will always remain in our memory. For the record, its height is 1472 feet, weight 365,000 tons, number of bricks to build it 10 million and it took just two years to build.

Now I come to report which was without doubt for me personally the hardest part of the entire marathon. It was a real killer of a walk and I had to draw on all my resources of strength and energy and what I had in reserve. I expected it to be tough but it exceeded all expectations. Oh how I cursed that bridge as I strove to beat the pain barrier and the bridge I refer to is the mighty steel structured Queensborough Bridge, the link that joins Queens with Manhattan. The Queensborough Bridge was opened in 1909 and it is also known as the 59th Street Bridge, made famous evidently by Simon and Garfunkel but that is another story. I started to climb up this rather steep incline round about the fifteen-mile point. My walk took me over the East River, also over the Roosevelt Island, and by the time I reached Manhattan I was quite exhausted and light-headed. I did feel at one stage I might pass out and I had aches in my body that never existed before. When I was halfway up this bridge the weather had changed considerably colder and I knew immediately why it has the reputation of being an unmerciful bridge to climb. I really could have surrendered to the inevitable, but I didn't. Since the marathon I have seen the video which a friend taped for me from Sky Television. The comments of the New Yorker correspondent who on being interviewed and who had previously run the marathon, made this interesting observation "The Queensborough Bridge offers the biggest and toughest challenge of the whole of the course to any athlete as he tackles a very steep hill on a lonely and cold bridge". On climbing that bridge, I thought of endless subjects to keep the concentration intact. At times I'd go off into my very own little world and think of England and I even questioned myself actually being there and not for the first time I might add.

So what were my deep inner thoughts as I battled to walk over that bridge. . First of all, I had to adapt a positive attitude by convincing myself I was so fortunate to be in good condition and that I could do it. Second was how incredibly lucky I've been all my life because I have never suffered any disability or illness of any sort, apart from the odd cold we all get occasionally. So if I was to moan or groan in any way, then I should be downright ashamed of myself. I have tried to adopt this attitude on all the marathons I've ever done and it seems to work. But human nature being what it is I moaned all right and the problems I had with my legs and feet seemed to multiply tenfold, so much so that the East River underneath the bridge looked so very tempting that I could quite easily have jumped in it.

When I joined the steady incline uphill of the Queensborough Bridge, it must have been nearly half a mile by the time I crossed over the bridge into Manhattan and to keep the concentration going I thought of the charity "Get Kids Going". I thought of little kids who in all probability are born disabled and have literally no use in their legs whatsoever. If that had happened to me, I certainly couldn't have played cricket and soccer and all the other sports I've played. How could I possibly have walked marathons without good legs. Little kids do not ask to be born into this world and what cruel luck to be born that way. How wonderful it is then for the "Get Kids Going" charity to be involved in raising money for disabled children so they can play sports while sitting in personalised wheelchairs . This charity really is giving children the wonderful opportunity of participating in sport but wheelchairs cost money and this was why I was competing in the marathon. Although my body discovered different aches and pains walking that bridge, I repeatedly vowed not to feel sorry for myself. To have sought sympathy in any way would have been defeatism. As regards raising money for "Get Kids Going", which incidentally applies to all my marathons, nothing would ever have been raised without the generosity of those who sponsored me.

Now when the going gets really tough on a marathon and I really mean tough, there's one such lady who accompanies me in my thoughts on all my marathons. This New York City Marathon was no exception. This very special lady in her own way is quite extraordinary and I have to say she is my inspiration for all the marathons I've ever done. I could weep for her every time I see her because her quality of life is nil. This lady has slumped, and I mean slumped, in a wheelchair for seventeen years. She has the dreaded motor neurone disease, the fatal disease that affects the motor neurones, the nerve cells, which connect the brain and spinal cord to the body's muscles. As the cells die the muscles weaken and begin to waste away. Average life expectancy is fourteen months after diagnosis. In most cases it is a swift, remorseful killer. The lady who has this incurable disease is Edna, who is my wife's sister. She cannot speak, feed herself, wash herself, dress herself or use the toilet herself as everything is done for her. There are the occasional motor neurone sufferers who may live for many years with this disease, and Edna is one of the longest sufferers of this disease in Great Britain and because of her I qualified to go in last year's London Marathon raising money through sponsorship for motor neurone. How she keeps going I'll never know but her will to live is strong so when the going is tough and the pain I experience on marathons gives me acute physical hurt, I shout to myself to stop whingeing and I think of Edna. That shouting I do partly releases me from any pain or trauma I may be experiencing and my problems are then put in its true and proper perspective. Edna is simply incredible. The frustration she must feel is so immense for me even to begin to comprehend. My advice for anyone feeling a bit low or sorry for themselves is to visit Edna. I promise you won't feel sorry with yourself for long.

On that bridge I also thought many times about my family. I've been blessed with a great wife – two children and three adorable grandchildren. I know my wife didn't want me to do this marathon, her main concern being would I be able to do it. With nearly forty years of marriage between us, she was naturally concerned that I was doing too much but I had such a burning desire to take part in this particular marathon. Also on that bridge, I thought of the Bull Hotel in Market Deeping. As this marathon was on a Sunday my thoughts invariably turned to Bert Murray's pub where most Sunday lunchtimes I indulge in a couple of pints. I know the time-scale was different in New York to England but it was Sunday lunchtime as I crossed that bridge and I really did think about those two pints, I really did. But any taste of alcohol would have finished my marathon. It's surprising though the amount of beer I am offered on marathons – New York being no exception. On walking by pubs I was forever being asked to have a drink by spectators. On marathons the temptation to drink a beer is all so powerful at times having used up so much energy, but to drink a beer would be sheet lunacy.

The slope coming off the Queensborough Bridge is very steep and bundles of straw had been put at the end of the slope to protect athletes from being injured because behind the straw is the metal construction of the bridge, which would have been very painful to have hit those metal girders for any athlete. I was so thankful for those bundles of straw because I actually fell into them because of the speed I came down that slope I couldn't stop myself. For one very split second I could have stayed down. It was, indeed, so heavenly but sheer willpower pulled me up and having completed sixteen miles in approximately six hours, I had still ten miles to go and here I was in Manhattan with a long stretch of four and a half miles which would eventually take me into the Bronx.

On First Avenue I was back to reality because for the previous three miles I'd hardly seen anyone. Roads and the Queensborough Bridge had still been closed to traffic and for long periods I was left completely on my own. I was still very much reliant on the smiling cops for directions. It seemed at times it was a one-man marathon effort but once over the bridge the situation had altered and with First Avenue being a very straight avenue I could actually see some walkers in front of me. Some of those walkers may well have been runners who had averted to walking the marathon, maybe because of some injury or possibly feeling unwell, or may even be on their last legs so to speak, but the loneliness of being the long distance marathon walker had left me at least for the time being. On First Avenue the crowds were back, certainly not as they were six hours previously because First Avenue would be packed with spectators to watch the early runners, but I once again had a spring in my step. The cold wind I'd felt on that massive steel bridge had left me and at seventeen miles I felt reasonably comfortable with small groups of spectators giving me every encouragement.

Water stations are a definite must at all marathons to keep fluid in the body. There are no water stations for three miles but once past that first three miles runners and walkers are then forever drinking water. The runners, of course, running at their speed just could not survive without water but that applies to all competitors as they often gasp for water every mile. These water stations consist of tables on both sides of the marathon course covered with cups of water. Sometimes helpful volunteers will stand in the front of the tables with a cup in their hands which, if anything, is probably easier for the athlete than taking it from the table. What the competitor doesn't do is stop to drink. As he runs by these tables he either takes one or is given one. The athletes might just take one sip of the water and throws the plastic cup to the ground. Consequently, when walkers like myself reach the water stations many hours later, the whole area is covered with these plastic cups which can be of some concern to the walker. I'm always frightened of these cups scattered over the roadside that I might slip over also because of the amount of water on the roads and the area can be very slippery.

Also on this marathon and always a most welcome sight, although one hopes never to have to use them, are the medical aid stations. I say welcome because if athletes were taken ill or sustained a serious injury there is at least someone along the marathon route who one can turn to for assistance. All sorts of problems can occur on a marathon. I know that going over the Queensborough Bridge and what that bridge took out of me. I did at one stage feel quite faint, and maybe I perhaps couldn't have continued any further, and it was consoling for me that first aid people were about. Medical aid stations are situated every four miles, usually behind water stations, so if one does incur an injury or feel discomfort at any time, notably cramp or blisters which often seem the most common cause, there are physicians, podiatrists and other medical personnel to help one. These first aid people do wonderful work who generally are most appreciated by all competitors of any marathon. I'm sure many athletes have a lot to thank medical aid stations for because without medical help some athletes would just not be able to finish the course.

Portable toilets are to be found every four miles on the marathon route. I have written previously about these toilets on Staten Island. These, in some instances, are probably as important as the water stations because they are constantly used and if the happenings of what went on at Staten Island were unpleasant to some, then what happens during marathons is considerably worse. At times there are long queues of runners waiting to use the toilets and their patience is sorely tested because they are losing valuable time and they can get very agitated. Because of the constant use of the toilets, they are dreadful places to use. The stench is quite revolting and they are left in a terrible condition. Pans are often overflowing with toilet paper and newspapers scattered everywhere. The doors to the toilets are invariably left open and once again the walker gets the worst of it. The walker obviously cannot get by those toilets at the speed a runner can, and there might be a dozen toilets all zoned together, so try to imagine the nauseating smell as the walker walks by them. I must add though that this situation is the same at all the marathons I've been involved in. As I walked by those toilets I was extremely thankful I didn't have to use them but just imagine if it was necessary for me to have used them and sat down (Heaven forbid) would I then have the strength to lift myself off the seat having walked sixteen miles. What a dreadful thought that is. Fortunately it was never put to the test.

I had rediscovered my walking rhythm and I was in the groove. At this particular point in the race I surprised myself how well my marathon was going and I actually overtook a couple of walkers who were both in serious trouble. One was limping so very badly that I knew he couldn't carry on much longer and further along First Avenue I saw one very elderly gentleman finally giving in to fatigue as he seemed to collapse into a waiting car. Because of the intense security, athletes had been instructed to take only food and water from the official race organisers instead of accepting food from unknown faces along the route. This was never a problem at water stations because all the people helping out there would be part of the vast organisation for the day. I suppose there was the fear that taking chocolate from some persons unattached to the marathon could lead to serious consequences for athletes. I can remember taking the odd sweet from a child on route and also once I was grateful for a half an orange. Generally, however, I didn't need to take anything from anyone because before the start of the marathon my belt pouch was stuffed with sweets and chocolates so I never go short because I'm a glutton for anything sweet.

The time was approximately 4.30 pm as I arrived at the seventeenth mile point and still for the umpteenth time I was being greeted with "Keep going Buddy" and being a late Sunday afternoon First Avenue was starting to come alive with the evening approaching. Attractive, young teenage American girls looked to be making for a night on the town as they made for the pubs and restaurants, which I noticed, were rapidly getting busier in this part of midtown Manhattan. These young girls, so stunning in their high heels, long legs and short skirts, made my tired heart and aching feet and legs feel good, and even they were giving me every encouragement, so often they seemed quite anxious to speak to me as they crossed the road on First Avenue deliberately making for me and often saying "How'ya doing Buddy". I must have looked highly embarrassed though when a large crowd of these girls who had congregated outside a pub burst into spontaneous applause as I passed them, followed by a series of wolf whistles, "it couldn't be my legs surely" I thought. I can also remember a group of young girls waving furiously and cheering me on from sky-rise buildings and wouldn't stop until I waved back. The lift in my spirits I was getting from those young girls was truly astonishing as all thoughts of tiredness quickly evaporated and I must have looked also so very conspicuous. This lone figure who was seemingly being allowed the freedom to walk right in the centre of First Avenue with those great cops still making allowances for me that nothing should stand in my way. It was as though out in the middle of First Avenue midtown Manhattan was mine. It was here that I burst into song again with "Give my regards to Broadway", it being most appropriate and so good for the concentration. I felt really satisfied with my progress and rejuvenated once more, and Manhattan really was mine.

Baseball, along with American football, is surely what the sports-loving American public is most interested in. Baseball has a huge following in the States and in many areas that I've walked through the marathon and on First Avenue, I've seen many kids playing the game. One cannot go far without seeing a game being played in a park somewhere. Baseball was first played in America in 1845 and since then the game has really took off, becoming hugely popular. If we in Great Britain think that soccer is big business, then it is small fry compared to baseball with players earning at least ten times as much as the average soccer players in the English Premier League. This also applies to American football stars and, of course, basketball. In New York the two most successful baseball sides are the New York Mets who play at the Shea Stadium in Queens and the New York Yankees who play at the Yankee Stadium in the Bronx. I would very much like to see a big baseball game just to satisfy my curiosity as to what the game is all about.

The excitement the game generates in the States is quite unbelievable and whilst I was in New York, the New York Yankees were playing the Arizona Diamond Backs in Phoenix for the World Series. The TV stations seemed to be covering all these matches which in New York created massive interest. The big upset was the Yankees losing in the finals. New York was devastated that their beloved Yankees could actually lose. On watching some of these matches on TV and out of curiosity, I wondered how the Americans would take to cricket. I'm sure cricket would appear to them a most foreign and boring sport because from what I've learnt about the American character is that they love instant excitement and entertainment in their sports, which they invariably get from watching baseball and American football. However, it is a fact and little known that there is a thriving cricket league in New York, generally made up of West Indians, Pakistanis and Indians who have settled there. As regards cricket being boring, I have to admit that even a seasoned cricket lover like myself can go to a packed Lords Cricket Ground in London to see a Test Match and sitting in the hot sun I can easily fall asleep. So if that can happen to me, then what chance have the Americans of understanding the game.

Evidently there is a fitness revolution going on in America with health and gymnastic clubs in demand with the emphasis very much on finding the correct exercise for the individual concerned. But one doesn't have to join a health club or whatever to be fit because the simple remedy to keep fit and, more importantly, to stay fit is by walking and the popularity of walking has increased tenfold in recent years in the States. During the marathon I came across many walkers walking in the opposite direction to me, not only were they saying "Keep going Buddy" but I immediately recognised them as the dedicated walkers which they undoubtedly are because of the long strides they take and walking at a brisk pace with head held high and arms swinging by their sides. I saw scores of these walkers, particularly on 1st Avenue, and they were not on a Sunday afternoon stroll either because they were in deep concentration in what they were doing and adapting a very positive attitude. They have obviously discovered the sheer joy of walking that I spoke of earlier in this book. I think what hasn't helped Americans is the enormous appetites some of them have. One has only to go in a restaurant in the States and see how their plates are piled up with food. Consequently the more one eats and not partaking in any kind of exercise at all, the quicker it will be to become overweight. Walking therefore is as popular as it has ever been in the States, which was very evident in New York. One doesn't have to play squash or take up jogging as one gets older to be fit because one could be on course for a heart attack. I guarantee that if people are concerned about their health with the increasing weight problems they may have, then my advice is to start walking. Just half a mile a day to start with and the pounds will drop off. It won't be easy at first but eventually one will enjoy it, then gradually increase on the mileage, that's if one wants to. Many Americans have discovered walking is a wonderful exercise and great for the heart and relaxation. Walking will have become an integral part of their lives and once in the body's system it can become an addiction. I know this to be the position with me because the physical activity of walking is so important as one gets older.

Suddenly on reaching the eighteenth mile point I felt so desperately tired and it's quite strange how this tiredness can suddenly strike. I knew it would come sooner or later. Because of this tiredness I sensed trouble ahead and I seemed to be hitting that invisible wall again. At this stage of the marathon I would have given my house away just for a good sit down. I then, and not for the first time, questioned myself as to what I was doing there. When one is tired and threatening to drop out of a marathon, all sorts of thoughts and problems come into the head. Why did I have to do this marathon I repeatedly asked myself. Surely having completed the London Marathon in April was enough for one year. I also thought of my family again because I knew they would be thinking of me. It was probably just as well they couldn't see me in view of the gruelling time I was going through. My wife was right because she had tried to convince me that two marathons in a year was just too much. I also realised on this marathon that it just wasn't the competing in two marathons, but the hundreds of hours I spent on my training walks. It was as though in the year 2001 I was forever walking.

Now the wall that was causing enormous problems really did feel as though I was pushing against some Berlin Wall as I strove to push through it. Yet again, I just had to stay positive with all negative thoughts once again disposed of. I again had to draw on my inner strength and resources to keep me moving. Hadn't well over two hundred and fifty people sponsored me for the marvellous "Get Kids Going" charity I asked myself? I couldn't let them down and even worse the charity I was doing it for, those poor disabled children needed my help to buy them a wheelchair. I knew immediately there could be no surrender and I also knew that it was my decision entirely to return to New York and walk the marathon. Any pain or discomfort I may have been suffering was very much of my own making. So I had no one to blame but myself. I knew the score and the consequences of failure. And yes it was me who had wanted to return to this most exciting of all cities and what better way for me to see New York was there than for me to walk through 26 miles of it but after 19 miles on the toughest of all marathons, it just didn't seem such a good idea any more.

With the Bronx in sight it was time for me to leave the area of North Manhattan known as Upper Side East. First Avenue had seemed an eternity as I experienced many highs and lows but somehow I had managed to recharge my batteries and had beaten the challenge of that wall. I can only assume that sheer willpower and obstinacy, together with an uncompromising stubbornness, saw me through it but never once did I yield to the continued temptation of enough is enough. It was mighty close, believe me. What had been a source of comfort was to pass the mile boards, which are situated every mile on the side of the avenues along the marathon route showing in large figures the amount of mileage done. Try to imagine my delight on seeing 20 miles on the board as I crossed over the River Harlem on the Willis Avenue Bridge. I was then in the borough of the Bronx with just six miles to go. I've cracked it I joyfully told myself but I must have been kidding because I know only too well from experience that the last six miles can undoubtedly be the worst with so much anguish and torment and fatigue.

What was fast becoming a problem though was that the day's light was quickly disappearing and if I didn't manage to keep up with the odd walker or two in front of me, then I could be in serious trouble without any sign of Race Marshalls and very few Police Officers left to give me directions. I would be at the mercy of the unpredictability of the Bronx. I say mercy because the Bronx has the reputation of being the toughest of the five boroughs and this reputation very much applies to South Bronx, the very area where I was walking and where juvenile delinquency ran amok not so long ago in the ghettos. Then the Bronx had a notorious image of decay and abandoned buildings with high crime figures, etc. A stranger walking through South Bronx on one's own a few years ago had a fair chance of being mugged, particularly at night, and this still applies today. But South Bronx is notably different. Now two years later and crime figures continue to fall. This has happened by a massive clampdown on crime in New York. Evidence now proves that you are more likely to be mugged or even beaten up in London than in New York and also in London well over 200 street crimes are committed every day. Not all the Bronx's population of 1.2 million live in poverty, however, because along the Hudson River going up to the Northern parts there are to be found elegant villas and beautiful mansions as good as any property seen in the five boroughs. Whilst walking through South Bronx I can honestly say I never at any time felt threatened in any way.

Because of the tough reputation that the Bronx once undoubtedly had, I thought about boxing as I walked through it. As one who had a few bouts himself in his youth, I've had more than a passing interest in the sport and because of the fight game I couldn't help but think of boxing champions from years past whose ambition when they were younger would have been to fight their way out of the ghettos they were born in. There would be densely populated slum areas which would be inhabited by social and economically deprived minorities and over the years many of boxing's greats have been born in such American slums. There was a saying way back in the thirties that a hungry fighter could become a great fighter and boxing was as good a way out as any for young teenage kids from escaping those notorious ghettos. It meant that if you were born poor and poor meant that often in the thirties and forties there was at times hardly anything to eat, that it would make a promising young boxer even more determined to succeed. So the fight game was always a natural outlet for deprived youngsters to hopefully earn some money and escape those appalling neighbourhoods. Admittedly I didn't see any ghettos during my short stay in the Bronx but it could be that the next world heavyweight champion might well come from one such neighbourhood.

I was walking through the Bronx less than an hour before I crossed over the River Harlem again, this time by the Madison Avenue Bridge. Having crossed over the last of the five bridges of the course, I felt I was getting somewhere. Strange is it not that when one visits an area or district for the very first time one might think of a certain name that one can associate with that area and on walking through Harlem there was only one name that I could associate with Harlem and that was the Harlem

Globetrotters. Ever since I was a boy I had heard of this world famous basketball team. The name was legendary as far as I was concerned. They are as equally well known as any baseball team or American football team in New York, where American giants of over seven feet tall have over the years dominated the sport, where its heroes have reached super star status with colossal earnings, making its players amongst the highest paid sports stars in the world. Having played basketball in the Army, I could never say it was one of my favourite sports but I certainly thought about the Harlem Globetrotters at that particular time and I wondered where their base would be in Harlem. But I've been informed on arriving home that the Harlem Globetrotters are not quite the formidable team they once were although they still play a lot of competitive matches throughout America. They now play many exhibition matches and have toured Great Britain regularly along with Europe, raising money for charities. Formed in 1936, a Mannie Jackson purchased the Globetrotters in 1993 and today they are more commonly known as Jackson's Globetrotters.

Being in Harlem and back on Manhattan Island, I was in Upper Side West of the borough with just five miles to go with the time on 6.00 pm. As I had feared earlier in the day, this particular marathon would take me longer than any other. That didn't necessarily bother me too much because my ambition was just to get round the course but the increasing problem for me and other walkers at the rear of the race was the constant fear of getting completely and hopelessly lost. When darkness descends it is twice as difficult to find a marathon route and I well remember taking a wrong turning to be told, fortunately, that I was on the wrong street by a local man. I quickly had to double-back. Try walking through the streets of any town or city when it is dark and where you have never been before, coupled with the fact that you are in a different country to your own. It was only through the kindness of local residents, who seemed to be going out of their way to give me directions as to where I should be making for since with my marathon gear on they could see I was one of the few remaining participants left in the race. If it had not been for them I wouldn't have a clue where I was going.

I am never quite sure that Marathon Officials quite realise what goes on at the rear of a marathon. It is as though all the interest is in the winners of the race and the early runners who finish and rightly so because there are cup presentations and large cheques given to the winners and obviously many congratulations given, watched by huge crowds with different television companies recording the event throughout America. But the strugglers, those runners who may have injured themselves, and the walkers seem to be fighting a long and lone battle of their own to stay in the marathon. I have actually seen athletes in various marathons in absolute agony because of an injury with not a first-aid man or race marshall in sight who might have given treatment or directions to the finish line. I do not make this a particular criticism of this New York City Marathon because so much of the marathon and general organisation has been superb, but it is as though the strugglers and walkers in all marathons are very much left on their own and most of these athletes are often people who raise vast amounts of money through sponsorship for charities and they are always at the rear of any marathon and so often completely on their own. I believe more consideration should be given to them. To me these people are the real heroes of any marathon but I have to accept that first aid people at the medical stations and the race marshalls are often volunteers who give up their valuable spare time freely at all marathons wherever they may be and I don't want to be seen to be critical of them.

After a short period where I virtually didn't see any people at all, I suddenly found myself in an extremely busy Fifth Avenue. This was a hive of activity with busy shops and shoppers galore, full of noisy and exhaust-fuelled vehicles in a blazing hurry, and where the yellow cabs are blatantly evident. These yellow cab drivers must know New York like the back of their hands as they go in and out of the busy streets, at times with great speed. I must admit to upsetting a few of them because of my own stupidity. Yes, I hold my hands up in apology because I nearly didn't finish the marathon at all. In fact, I was most fortunate because I could quite easily have been knocked down, not just by a yellow cab but also by a bus as I tried to cross over a very highly active street on Fifth Avenue. The only comparison I can compare with what happened to me is of trying to evade the dodgems in the fairground. When one is isolated in the centre in total bewilderment and chaos and trying to escape with unfortunately nowhere to run to, that's exactly what happened to me.

In Manhattan nearly all the roads going North or South are Avenues and the roads going off the avenues are called streets, with the streets always being at right angles to the avenues, which go from East to West. The problem was that when I was walking along the pavements of Fifth Avenue, I was forever bumping into someone because there were so many people about. Also, at just about every three or four hundred yards, I would come across a street and waiting on the pavements for the lights to go green tested my patience. Because of the crowds waiting, it meant I was losing valuable time, which also meant, of course, that my marathon would take even longer. I might add that at this so annoying time I was getting quite irritable with what was happening. I was tired and I wanted this marathon well and truly finished. But now with all the traffic back to normal it meant that I was just an ordinary pedestrian just like everyone else. There was certainly no more holding up of traffic for me and because those police officers had been so considerate to me previously, often stopping the traffic for me, that I must have taken advantage of that when I tried to cross over 126th Street. The red traffic light for pedestrians was giving the signal NO and I really was taking a hell of a chance with my life. But my mind was so wrapped up in completing the marathon I wasn't thinking of anything else and I must have been in a dream because here was I stranded in the middle of a very busy street indeed with fast motor vehicles flying by either side of me. The yellow cab drivers with windows open were shouting abuse at me and with a bus bearing down on me at such speed that I can say without hesitation that it was curtains for me. Fortunately, the driver saw me just in time as he ground to a halt causing vehicle horns to be blown all around. The bus driver was violently shaking his head in obvious annoyance at me and I apologised profusely with my hands. Anyone who has seen New York's traffic will tell you that if as a pedestrian you cross over one of these busy streets when the red light is on, you are definitely putting your life at risk. When I think of that incident many months later, I can still break out in a cold sweat. How could I have been so utterly careless? I may have done some real stupid things in my lifetime and that was certainly one of them.

I passed the mile board with twenty-three miles showing and I was still on Fifth Avenue, which would eventually take me to Central Park. I think at this stage of the marathon I seemed oblivious to any discomfort or anguish as I dragged my aching body along. My ankle was giving me regular twinges of acute pain, an aching pain that restricted me somewhat because of my limping. On looking down at my ankle, I was putting my foot down at right angles to my body, anything to keep the momentum going with the finish not far away. It was then in the darkness under the Avenue's lighting that I saw a fireman just ahead of me. I had trailed behind this fireman several times during the marathon. He would increase his speed and I would lose him for a while but he was really struggling to keep moving as I gradually caught up with him. I had seen this fireman earlier in the day at Staten Island, he being most noticeable in his fireman's clothes and helmet. This was how he had walked his marathon, properly dressed as if he was required to go and put out a major fire in the city. Now this man was a hero to me because here he was a New York City Fireman walking in this marathon for colleagues who perished in the Twin Towers. Three hundred and thirty-four firemen had lost their lives. It honestly does not bear thinking about and it seems hardly imaginable that so many firemen could be killed in one day.

I was determined to speak to this fireman, if only to give him some encouragement, which I felt he desperately, needed. As we stood side by side on Fifth Avenue with the lights on red waiting to cross over 110th Street, I said to him:

"How are you buddy?" I surprised myself by addressing him in such an American way.

"Not good" he said. I believed this to be his reply.

That was all the conversation I could get from him as I continued to look at him. He was wobbling slightly and I thought he was going to collapse. It looked as though he couldn't possibly go any further and I tried to offer him words of comfort. He really did look in a very distressed state but, unfortunately for him, I had my own problems on nearing twenty-four miles because I was up against that wall again and I was in no condition to help anyone. When the lights showed green, I moved ahead of him leaving him in a very confused and unstable way. As I sit now in the comfort of my home writing the memories of an unforgettable day, I bitterly regret that decision. In fact, in really guilty moments, I feel quite ashamed of myself that I didn't get hold of his arm and that way the two of us could have walked to the finish line together. When I left him at those traffic lights I was thinking of my own personal feelings, which were selfish to say the least. I had looked upon this fireman as a real hero and just when he needed my helping hand, I didn't' give it. I've thought many times about this fireman since I arrived home. I never did know whether he was successful or not in finishing the marathon. I sincerely hope he was because if anyone deserved to complete the race it was him. New York City should be proud of that fireman for what he did that day and, for entirely different reasons, when he needed my help and being unable to give it I am never likely to forget that man either.

I make no apologies or excuses that during the marathon I did try to seek divine intervention from above. Certainly during long periods of difficulties and distress when I was suffering arduous and laborious times, especially going over the Queensborough Bridge and at the end of First Avenue and definitely the last five miles of the race. As I've got great faith these days it means that my religion is very important to me so it was such a natural thing for me to do and because of what I was putting my body through, I thought of India where the Ursuline Sisters of Bihar are to be found. During a visit to their Convent school a few years ago, I was plagued by back problems and in terrible pain. These sisters had told me then that whatever the amount of pain I was experiencing, that God loved me and the greater the pain, the greater He loved me. I tried to console myself with those words and that hopefully He would help me in this marathon. Well, I was in pain all right and I so desperately needed His help to keep me going. My stamina seemed to be decreasing at an alarming rate as this so tortuous marathon became increasingly harder the longer it went on.

On at last approaching the Northern end of Central Avenue, a walker whom I'd followed for some time suddenly collapsed and fell on to the pavement. I thought he had been swaying considerably and by the time I caught up with him he was lying on a garden seat in front of a shop. He looked in a positively awful state and was near exhaustion with a deathly white look on his face. He was probably about my age and fortunately he was being attended to by the shop owner as I proceeded on.

I also came across a runner who because of pulling a muscle in his leg, he was reduced to walking and I could see the sheer torment he was putting himself through as every step he took was a supreme effort by him. But his determination was such that failure for him didn't come into it. All athletes were showing this "United we run" spirit but it is surprising what the human body can take and there was no giving up for athletes who have trained for months. So whether it's illness, which includes being sick from the throwing up of all the sheer amount of water which has been drunk or injury, there's no giving up, even more so when one is three miles from the finish. I am reminded of what a young Mother had to say to me a few years ago while walking the London Marathon together for the last eight miles of the race. We were both struggling with fatigue and the going was tough. She said "A marathon is like having a baby, in great agony at times but so incredibly happy when it's all over".

So here I am in the very centre of this great city as I strive to go the last half a mile on Fifth Avenue to the East Side entrance of Central Park. So alone was I that it was just incredible that there was literally no one about and I was not just thinking about the athletes, it was rather weird that to my left were huge skyscrapers, which incidentally surround Central Park, and to my right was the park itself. This quietness in New York of all places takes some believing with so little traffic about. Also, maybe being Sunday evening had something to do with it. Yet only hours before this very same avenue would have been boiling over with fanaticism and intensity with huge crowds cheering on the eventual winners. How I could have done with some of those crowds to give me that lift I so desperately needed. At that very moment, those early runners would probably be wallowing in celebration of their achievements many hours earlier. How I envied them as I delved ever deeper into my reserves of energy as it did cross my mind that this could be my last marathon. If that was so, then the New York City Marathon was as good a one as any to finish with. But just when I thought the whole of the city was asleep, there was the welcome sight of the Race Marshals at last, near 86th Street, waiting to direct me into Central Park.

"Well done and keep going Buddy. You're nearly there," they said. That remark was music to my ears. Also, knowing that I had made it to Central Park and with new found enthusiasm and so it seemed energy, I straightened my back, pulled myself together and swung my arms, knowing that I'd got just over two miles to go. It was 7.45 pm on my wrist-watch and having walked twenty-four miles, there was simply no way I wasn't going to do it.

Once in Central Park I found a certain serenity with the stillness and of the evening there and once again apart from the odd jogger or cyclist, the park seemed empty. At this point I planned my final assault as it were on the remaining two miles and my enthusiasm got the better of me when I tried to walk quicker. Alas I couldn't but in the very beautiful Central Park it was definitely "Autumn in New York" time again and with a burst of energy in my lungs, I sang that ballad again. It didn't matter who was in that park as I sang as loudly as I possibly could. The startled looks I got from the odd walkers going for an evening stroll was surprising to say the least. How I loved it in that park. All tiredness had gone and I felt exhilarated. It seemed so fitting, so proper and so appropriate that I of all people should wake up the peacefulness of Central Park in my celebration of just being there and "Autumn in New York" was very real indeed. The intense excitement of knowing that the finish was not too far away meant that I was coming home.

Evidently not so many years ago Central Park used to be a muggers' paradise but with the severe crackdown by police on crime in the city, the park is comparatively safe. But only during daytime because at night it is a highly dangerous place indeed. Never venture into the park at night, particularly on your own, I'd read before I came to New York. So, say I had been challenged and some mugger had demanded money from me, what condition would I have been in to defend myself? The answer must be none whatsoever because although I seemed to have discovered renewed energy, I really was as weak as a kitten. In fact, a gust of wind would have knocked me over and all I had on my person was a few sweets. But I certainly wasn't thinking about being mugged as I continued along those tree-lined driveways where during the day horse-drawn carriages would carry passengers to explore the delights of the park. New Yorkers love Central Park where well-known celebrities live in their luxurious flats which reach for the sky overlooking the park. John Lennon of The Beatles was murdered outside one such place, which is known today as Strawberry Fields. Central Park is a stretch of greenery of some 843 acres and one would have to travel many miles out of the city to find a greenbelt area comparable. Wise men of New York made a decision that in 1856 a large public park was needed for the city, preferably in the middle of Manhattan. And so it was and its popularity is immense and New York would never be the same without Central Park

Everything was going along just fine and with this new surge of self-motivation I felt once again reasonably confident I would do it. With just a mile to go, however, I had inconveniently hit the wall again. I have never hit that so and so wall so many times in any of my previous marathons and here I was trying to overcome such heights of stubbornness within my body that I seemed to be asking the near-impossible to accomplish what I'd set out to achieve hours before. Hadn't I trembled with excitement on the Verrazano Narrows Bridge that morning where I was surrounded by thousands of athletes? What prolific stimulation that had been to my nervous system as my confidence was sky-high after Rudy Giuliani's rousing send-off speech. All that seemed an eternity away. In fact, it seemed such a long time ago that it had seemed like yesterday as I looked back on the earlier events of the day. But at this most crucial moment of the whole race, after having walked twenty-five miles, I was in crisis as I was hurting like never before. Fatigue had hit me like lightning and I thought that the Queensborough Bridge was energy-sapping enough but with just a mile to go I did have grave doubts as to whether I could do it. "Don't you dare give up now" I growled at myself in a bullying way. I'm sure that feeling so exhausted I could have curled up under the nearest tree in Central Park and slept for a week. To have sat down and rested my legs would have been pleasurable beyond words. It would be Utopia.

To get me from the very depths of dejection and despair I needed a lift of gigantic proportions to help me complete the last mile. It proved to be the longest mile of my life and I realised it was an endurance test of some magnitude. Again, I could have felt so sorry for myself as I had plunged to an ultimate low but positive I must be. Yet again I had to convince myself how considerably fortunate I was to be in this marathon and whatever pain I was suffering, it was only temporary compared to the terrible loss of life on September 11th. It was thinking of the Twin Towers and one last endeavour that I drew ever closer to the finish line. I shouted to myself to keep going and it helped enormously that I could bring my frustrations out into the open and out into the open meant Central Park. Whether anyone heard me or not it didn't really matter. I really was past caring and to avoid any sympathy to the predicament I was in, I list just some of the things I would have said to myself with half a mile to go:

"How would you like to be in Edna's situation where she has been slumped in a wheelchair for seventeen years and totally reliant on others to help her? How would you cope with that?""

"Stop whingeing and consider yourself extremely lucky you ungrateful idiot."

"Think of those children without legs for whom the 'Get Kids Going' charity is trying to raise money so they can buy wheelchairs in order for children to partake in sport. Soon you will be resting your tired and aching legs. Those disabled children haven't even got legs to rest."

"You are indeed one hell of a fortunate person. You were born with wonderful parents into quite a privileged middle-class family. Never at any time have you suffered any serious illness or injury and even today you still have a great life."

"You selfish buffoon. Your small problems are nothing in comparison to nearly a third of the world's population. Just think of those millions of Indian kids you saw when you visited India who are scavenging rubbish tips and begging on the streets in their thousands to avoid starvation. Those same thousands have no parents, no home, no money, no school and no hope. Don't you ever forget it, you have everything in comparison".

On having been so critical of myself and getting it off my chest so to speak, I sensed a slight feeling of hope and this happened towards the end of my stay in Central Park because very gradually I felt I had once again defeated that confounded wall. The sheer obstinacy of the unmerciful and often savage human barrier I had once again overcome and I knew the old enthusiasm was returning. This I believe was also partly due to those evening walkers in the park who were becoming increasingly more evident as their numbers increased, which meant that even more people were giving me their support that I so desperately needed. Those familiar and simple words of "Keep going Buddy" were being extended to "Keep going buddy, not long now". Those words really did hearten my heart at that precise moment. Maybe these people were giving me some sort of sympathy at the surprise of seeing someone still competing in the marathon, having probably thought the marathon had finished hours before, which of course it had for thousands earlier in the day. Perhaps they also thought I was surely the last marathoner still in the race but I knew I wouldn't be the last unless those few remaining strugglers behind me had given up. But as I've written previously in this book, just to have completed the marathon was my sole ambition. The accomplishment of the successful conclusion of the race was paramount for me as I drew ever closer to the finish.

The marathon route then took me briefly out of Central Park and back into Fifth Avenue and at last I really did feel I was in the hustle and bustle of New York City with plenty of people about who were encouraging me on. As those pavements ran parallel to the park, I could gradually see the entrance on the south side which would take me into Central Park again. Then it was a sharp turn right leaving

Fifth Avenue and into Central Park South and I knew I'd got less than ¹/₂ a mile to go and it was here that a middle aged lady rushes over from a small crowd of spectators with a large paper bag in her hands "Please take some raisins, they are good for you and will keep the energy going" she said in her American voice.

So here was I eating raisins purely on the advice of a woman whom I'd never met before. I had disregarded the warning that all the competitors should refrain from taking anything from anyone who was likely to offer refreshments of any sort but this lady was so persuasive in her insistence that raisins would be good for me and I was in no position to argue with her. In truth, I have to say, I had forgotten what I'd previously been told. She was then joined by her male partner and they accompanied me through to the finish, which I appreciated because I was not only getting a constant supply of raisins but the conversation the three of us were making helped me considerably. They will never know the value of that short chat with them. Their kindness and helpfulness is something I will never forget.

On approaching the main entrance to Central Park, temporary stands had been built which no doubt were full to capacity hours before and in those virtually empty stands there would still be the occasional spectator standing up and clapping as I walked by and on walking through the main entrance to the park I was greeted by large and small groups of people not only clapping but cheering. This did wonders for me as many shouted "You're nearly there Buddy". On re-entering Central Park I was again struck by the beautiful serenity of the place itself, such peacefulness is hard to imagine in such a big city. I immediately noticed how superior the lighting was than on the East side of the park and because of this additional lighting I knew I was on the last phase of a long journey. As I took another mouthful of raisins, all tiredness and physical injuries seemed to have evaporated from me, if only temporarily I might add. I braced myself for one final effort with less than a quarter of a mile to go. I really did feel I was coming home.

The very small concern for me to go that short distance to the finish was the very slight sloping hills in the park and when one has walked nearly 26 miles those hills can seem more than just slight. Nothing to worry about normally of course but the back of my legs felt real pressure on them to do this climb. But the spectators in Central Park, and there were still a few about, continued to urge me on. Then some marathoner was fast overtaking me who seemed to have come from nowhere. This competitor had made a successful late challenge and to the cheers of the small groups of onlookers he breezed by me. How I envied him his energy because I, incidentally, was not in any condition to contest that challenge. My priority was always to complete the race, not to have a do or die effort with some competitor as to who would defeat whom.

So my New York City Marathon, which had started on Staten Island nearly 8^1/$_2$ hours previously, was finally coming to its conclusion and through the Autumn trees of Central Park and walking on those quite lovely tree-lined pathways, I could at last see the bright lights that lit up the whole of the finish area. With the excitement multiplying every step of the way I could hear music and could see pockets of people standing about and even the race officials waiting to greet me at the finish. What on earth must the atmosphere have been like as the winners of this marathon entered Central Park hours earlier with thousands of spectators cheering them on? But winner or not, I would not give up what I was experiencing for anything and on again passing temporary built stands, I was receiving the warmest of welcomes from a few people still in those stands. Their applause really was a bit special. The finishing line beckoned as I tried to quicken my pace by swinging my arms in defiance of the tiredness. The adrenaline was pumping once more. I had done the Big Apple Marathon. No words from me now can describe how I really felt but I know that this is what dreams are made of, this would be the one to tell my grandchildren about. I felt deliriously happy as I hit the tape with a race official saying "Well done Buddy".

As I came through the tape I was quickly told by the race officials that my official marathon time to complete the course was 8 hours, 25 minutes and 58 seconds and amongst many congratulations I then had a silver heat sheet, as it is called, placed around my body in order to keep me warm. I was then helped by a couple of young ladies whose ages would be early twenties who had on their track suits the name of the New York Runners Club. They would be volunteers like the rest of those race officials. These two girls, so kind and caring in their attitude to me, could see I was well the worse for wear and although exhilarated I did feel extremely tired. But more than anything else, I just had to sit down. Whether I would ever be able to get up again I did not know or even care, but sit down I must. At that very moment a race official comes over to me. "Sorry Buddy but we forgot to give you your race medal" he says. Normally it is one of the first things that happens once over the finish line that the race medal is placed over the head. "How could I possibly return to England without my New York City Marathon medal? Nobody would have believed I'd done it" I said as this race official places the medal over my head. The medal was obviously most important to me which I knew would be pride of place at home. "Don't forget your baggage bag, you have to walk about a $1/4$ of a mile to get it. You will soon find the lorry where it is" he says, this being the lorry which had transported my baggage bag with my personal belongings from Staten Island earlier in the day.

"You see that seat over there, I'm going to sit down and I'm definitely not going to walk another ¼ mile that's for sure" I say. "But you've got to collect it Buddy, you really have" he says. "I'm going nowhere" I say in a defiant way. I didn't want to appear unreasonable to this race official but I was shattered as I slumped down in that Central Park garden seat. I honestly couldn't walk any further. "I'll go for him" says one of the young ladies and to my relief she rushes off to get my baggage bag which had my tracksuit inside and as it was getting notably colder I needed that tracksuit.

On sitting down with the other young lady who I might add was giving me her undivided attention, she being so concerned that I must keep warm and that I was to drink plenty of fluids of which she was giving me a regular supply, also on feeling hungry she gave me a bread roll which I munched like a horse who hadn't had any food for days. I was so hungry and apart from sweets and chocolates which I'd had on the marathon that was it. So on waiting for the other young lady to return with my baggage bag, I kept munching the bread rolls and got involved with this young lady who sat with me in conversation which clearly reflected the horrifying events of September 11th. She told me her name was Barbara and if I heard correctly she worked at the United Nations building in New York City which explains why she had a foreign accent. Our conversation is still clearly printed in my mind and even if I can't remember every word for word, I can assure the reader I'm fairly near to it. But I made an appalling gaffe with this girl and perhaps one should not divulge too much when speaking to a complete stranger but September 11th was very much on everyone's mind during my short stay in New York. The subject wouldn't go away and while talking to young Barbara it was inevitably brought up.

"You did well to get round the course and how are you

feeling now?" she asked.

"I feel fine but very tired, but in view of what happened on September 11th I just knew I had to complete that marathon" I said.

"Yes, I live and work in the city. It was a terrible experience for everyone, not just for those poor people who died but for everyone who lives here. I'm still in shock. I still can't believe it, and New York is in mourning and nothing here will ever be the same again" she said.

"I think the reason it shocked America so much was the Americans just didn't think that such a dreadful act of terrorism could happen in their own country" I said.

"America was under prepared, that was the problem" she says.

"In my country England we have lived under the constant fear of terrorism, particularly London. We have to be vigilant at all times. Terrorists can strike at any time, as has been the situation for many years now in the UK" I said.

"Just look at the Irish problem and the IRA, your country has certainly had its share of terrorism" she says.

"Terrorism has to be defeated otherwise democracy, the very fabric of our society, is ruined" I said.

"That's true" she says.

"Look how Great Britain suffered during the last war. Thousands killed and cities bombed by Germany. We had to defeat the aggressor. America had never before experienced anything like that" I said.

"Incidentally Barbara, where are you from?" I asked.

"I'm from Germany" she says.

I distinctly felt uncomfortable when she answered my question but how was I to know where she was born. We were just two people indulging in quiet conversation concerning what happened on September 11th, a day that shook the world and caught America off guard. We were then joined by the other young lady who had retrieved my baggage bag. Barbara was so concerned that I should get my tracksuit and sweater on as quickly as possible. No I hadn't offended her and she was just as caring as ever. The girls continued to get more clothes on me and I told them not to bother with my trainers as they seemed to literally be glued to my feet in view of that tightness. Once off my feet I knew I would never get them on again. I could quite easily have sat on that garden seat in Central Park for hours. It was without doubt the most comfortable wooden seat I'd ever sat on and the tranquillity of the park could have sent me off into a deep sleep. The self satisfaction of achievement is something only marathoners would understand, just ask any of those athletes who completed that marathon what their real feelings were on having done it. Of all the sports I've played, nothing can quite match up to the quite magnificent accomplishment of what one attains on the completion of a marathon. Please take my word for it. Nothing comes near it in comparison.

The two girls finally get me on my feet and I shuffle, with Barbara's help, out of Central Park. Outside of the park she was trying to wave a taxi for me but to no avail. New York's traffic seemed oblivious to a young lady trying to wave down a yellow cab. All this time I was leaning against a wall totally unable to help in any way and completely reliant on Barbara to get me a taxi. Finally, after some considerable time, a taxi pulls over to the kerb and Barbara informs the driver to take me to the Wellington Hotel. "The taxi is paid for by the New York Runners Club" she says as she shuts the passenger door. "All the best" she says as the taxi speeds away into the night. Without that girl's help goodness knows how I'd have made it back to my hotel. What an absolute smasher she was, not only in her looks but also in her so concerning disposition. She was just one such person who made my New York City

Marathon. I shall not forget her either.

After the short taxi journey to my hotel I managed to stumble out of the taxi and made my way to the hotel lift. Fortunately, I didn't see any of the runners who had been in the marathon because I would have been obliged to have asked them how they had got on, but I was too exhausted to speak to anyone. Once in my bedroom there was Nick in a very relaxed mood lying on his bed and he seemed reasonably pleased with the way his marathon had gone. He actually ran the marathon in 4 hours 19 minutes and considering this was his first ever marathon, this was excellent time, and having informed me that he enjoyed the marathon where obviously he had his bad periods like every athlete does. He then without hesitation quickly told me that he would definitely not be running another. It was probably something he had always wanted to do and having done it, that was it. He was quite adamant when he said "one is enough for me" but completing 26 miles 385 yards is, in my opinion, a test of one's character and Nick had undoubtedly passed his test. I hope also I hadn't disappointed him too much by informing him I was in no condition whatsoever to celebrate our success in Rosie O'Grady's pub. Say, for example, I had made it there and what condition would I have been in? There was a fair chance he would have to piggyback me on our return to the Wellington Hotel, not because of the drink but because of one extremely tired marathoner.

All I wanted on arriving at the hotel was a hot bath. The very thought of a hot bath can quite often keep one going during those very dark periods of any marathon and I know all marathoners will surely agree that to indulge in that lovely feeling of hot water around such a wearied and fatigued body is the ultimate in the way of relaxation. Having pushed and shoved the body through such unreasonable demands, where a hundred aches and pains throughout the body will gradually and hopefully fade away, a hot bath can quite easily have the effect of being drowsy and one could fall into a deep and satisfying sleep as one sinks lower and lower in the water. Usually I have the terrible problem of getting out of the bath after any marathon, when my son will invariably lift me out as I am so reliant on him to do so. In New York, however, my son wasn't with me and I knew I had to make the supreme effort of getting out of the bath myself. I'm sure Nick didn't realise the torment and predicament I had with the relatively simple procedure of getting out of the bath, but make it I did with great difficulty I might add. Otherwise I could quite easily have spent the night there.

After catching up on both our experiences of the marathon, Nick and I decided on an early night and bed beckoned provided, of course, I could sleep. Surely after walking over 26 miles sleep would have been the least of my troubles but my sleeping habits are far more complicated an issue than that as I proceeded to take the sleeping tablets. Having taken them for more years than I care to remember, they are well and truly in my system. The reason I have such difficulty in sleeping after a marathon is that I literally cannot keep my legs still as I am forever kicking and twitching all night through – just ask my wife. It's as though I am reliving the marathon again step by step and on having taken the sleeping tablets, I can at least stay reasonably still throughout the night and in my deep and satisfying sleep, even the noise from New York's traffic didn't awaken me.

I would like to think that on the night of the marathon I dropped off to sleep with a smile on my face because although exhausted one second, I felt exhilarated the next. Such contentment I felt throughout my mind and body is hard to define and I'd achieved that ambition of having completed the New York City Marathon. If it was meant to be my last marathon, I couldn't have timed it better and even more pleasing was that I could help the "Get Kids Going" charity. When all my sponsorship money is collected in, those kids will hopefully get their wheelchair. May I add finally, I wouldn't have exchanged my experiences of that Autumn day in New York, good and bad, for anything. All the money in the world couldn't replace how I was feeling.

Chapter Three

Autumn in New York

Although it was a reasonable night's sleep, I couldn't actually say it was a good one. I remember sleeping soundly to about 4.00 am but from then onwards I was getting regular disturbances by the continued process of going to the toilet, obviously being from the sheer amount of water consumed during the marathon. But I do know that when I hit the pillow I was dead to the world. If my legs were re-living the marathon then I was not aware of it but I had managed some sleep so I was grateful for that and at the breakfast table Nick and I ate a hearty breakfast. It's always the same for me after any marathon because my appetite is enormous. I suppose the loss of a substantial amount of weight can exceed many pounds so with the eating of several rounds of toast I was only trying to put back what I'd lost the previous day. I feel here that I may have an advantage being a walker than a runner. To run a marathon an athlete has to be superbly fit and if he or she wishes to keep the same weight, which often they do, then the over indulging of food after a marathon will quickly lead to putting weight on. I admit to carrying a few extra pounds at times but the runner, if they are serious with their running, will always carefully watch their weight after a marathon because they are often to be seen out on their daily training runs most evenings of the week, perhaps in preparation for another marathon somewhere. But for a walker like myself it is different and that morning at the breakfast table I was eating away quite merrily and heartedly with the thought that if I did indulge over excessively it didn't matter too much because with my daily walking I could soon lose any surplus weight when I arrived

Some of the 'Get Kids Going' competitors gather in the Mayfair Hotel in Manhattan, the evening before the marathon (note arrow for author).

The Wellington Hotel in 5th Avenue, Manhattan where the author and many competitors in the marathon stayed.

Runners gather on the Verrazano Narrows Bridge on Staten Island for the start of the 2001 New York City Marathon.

Runners cross the Verrazano Narrows Bridge at the start of the marathon from Staten Island to Brooklyn.

Some of the estimated 25,000 runners crossing over the Verrazano Narrows Bridge.

A runner holding a U.S. flag crosses the Verrazano Narrows Bridge.

At the very top of the Verrazano Narrows Bridge the skyline of Manhattan is visible in the far distance.

On 1st Avenue Jane Emmerson, Chief Executive of 'Get Kids Going' and marathon organiser with two staff colleagues.

It was estimated that 3 million spectators lined the marathon route, and this blank space was originally reserved for a photograph I was hoping to obtain of the leading runners running through the crowded avenues of Manhattan, but unfortunately I was unable to acquire any such photograph. What I did notice however while walking the marathon was that the occasional runner often had their own camera with them and actually took photo's while running the race. This being most noticeable during the first few miles, I did consider the possibility of actually carrying a camera myself because the Manhattan sky-line is positively mesmerising with a majesty all its own and I'm sure I could have taken some stunning photographs on such a momentous and emotional day, but I'm also equally sure that during the latter stages of an exhausting marathon I would literally be too weak to have carried even the smallest of camera's.

The unknown New York City Fireman in his firefighters gear pictured at the start of the Marathon walking for colleagues lost in the Twin Towers, 'what a man,' 'what a hero.' I finally drew level with him on Fifth Avenue waiting to cross over 110th Street having completed 23 miles.

"How are you buddy?" I ask.

"Not good," I believe he replied.

He looked dreadful and in a collapsed state, and I had my own problems because I was up against that invisible wall again, he needed my help and being selfish I left him totally alone on that crossing. I still feel guilty about that incident because I should have stayed with him. I never did know his name.

The only photograph of the author taken on the marathon, but the important one, arms still swinging as he crosses over the finish line in Central Park. Note the official time he took to walk the 2001 New York City Marathon.

home.

As regards the marathon, Nick and I had the most wonderful satisfaction of having completed it. It really is the most brilliant of feelings as one reflects on the enormity of what one has done and any pain or suffering experienced in the marathon had quickly receded. It's quite remarkable that having gone through so much trauma, anguish and downright pain that although somewhat drained we had surprised ourselves by how well we felt and over the breakfast table the marathon was the main topic of conversation. In the reception area of the hotel a Yorkshireman told me that the marathon was his sixth New York City Marathon and it was by far the toughest marathon he had ever participated in, saying that the heat of the day was quite overwhelming. "I've never known it so hot in New York for this time of the year" he had said. I really couldn't disagree with his observation of the race and other runners who had run the marathon told me also that they had experienced tough and laborious times. I got some consolation from those remarks being made and obviously I wasn't the only one who had struggled to complete the course. I was not sure what the temperature was at the hottest part of the day but those runners far more experienced in marathons than I'm ever likely to be had sweated bucketsful in order to complete the New York City Marathon.

What was a relief was that I could walk reasonably well because when I finally managed to remove the boot from my right foot after the marathon my ankle had seemed to have swollen up out of all proportion. I just hoped I hadn't done any serious damage. Nick and I decided that morning to revisit the finish line area of the marathon in Central Park, dare I say the scene of our triumph. I'm sure that if we did feel some smug satisfaction on a personal basis it was perhaps understandable. Believe me when I say that the pleasure of having completed a marathon can last for several days afterwards. It's as though one is on a permanent high and in Central Park that morning it was Autumn in New York time again, not that I sang the Sinatra classic because I had no intention of emptying that park on such a beautiful morning but the serenity of the park was still very evident amongst those Autumn trees with their falling leaves and I know that finishing a marathon there will forever be a special place to me because standing on the finish line that morning in Central Park I had a thousand memories of a quite memorable day that just wouldn't leave me.

As it had already been established that my official marathon finish time was 8 hours, 25 minutes, 58 seconds my net finish time was 8 hours, 22 minutes, 6 seconds, making a difference of 3 minutes, 52 seconds, less than my official time; the net reading being taken from my chip which had been tied to my foot. So I'm inclined to think the net time was the correct time. I list a few statistics for which I've got nothing at all to boast about. I suppose if I was more serious about my walking purely on a competitive basis these statistics could make depressing reading but my ambition had been to complete the marathon and as I was unable to go any faster there was literally nothing I could do about it. It wouldn't have bothered me if I'd finished last, I would still have had the feeling of exhilaration and triumph. (What an unusual boast that would be though, to say that I'd come last in the New York City Marathon).

> My overall placement in the marathon was 23,649 out of 23,664 total finishers, 15 finished behind me.
> My placement in the 65 – 69 age group being 203 out of 204.
> Placement by gender, 16804 out of 16811 male finishers.

My average pace per mile being 19 minutes, 17 seconds.
My first 13 miles, 3 hours, 46 minutes, 22 seconds.
My second 13 miles, 4 hours, 79 minutes, 36 seconds.

The winner of the marathon was Tesfaye Jifar of Ethiopia. Jifar fought off a strong Kenyan challenge and he became the first Ethiopian to win the New York City Marathon and the first woman home was Margaret Okayo of Kenya. Both these athletes set course records. Jifar completed the marathon in 2 hours, 6 minutes, 49 seconds and what was a surprise was that he had never won a marathon anywhere in the world before. Jifar's victory meant that he collected $130,000 which is obviously a huge amount of money for an athlete to win from the African continent. In sixth position for the order of finish in the men's race was a Jon Brown of Great Britain who completed the marathon in 2 hours, 11 minutes, 21 seconds. He is to be congratulated because Britain's record is not all that impressive in the men's marathons at present.

Remember Abraham Weintraub, the ninety-one year old runner who after just seven miles so casually overtook me in the marathon being accompanied by two teenage girls either side of him. Well I had the supreme satisfaction of reaching the finish line 8 minutes before him (surely it's not such a big deal that I can actually finish a marathon in front of a ninety-one year old pensioner). It was strange though that I must have overtaken him at some point but I couldn't remember having done so. Perhaps he was putting his feet up somewhere. If there were two people whom I admired in the marathon it was him and the unknown fireman. These two amongst countless others were the real heroes of the marathon.

What has sometimes slightly annoyed me in these world famous marathons, which are staged in various countries throughout the world, are the professionals who travel the world to participate in all the top marathons and if they are good enough, which they undoubtedly are, they will continue to take the prize money. Not only did Tesfaye Jifar benefit with this big cheque, and I also know that the winner of the last London Marathon, an American, picked up a winner's cheque for nearly £200,000 but the winning of any of the top marathons is not just about the winner receiving a lucrative cheque, but the spin off for something bigger from sponsorship, sports companies, those associated with athletics will pay thousands of pounds to have the winner's name involved with their company providing, of course, that the athlete will advertise the company's sports clothes and wear the company's sports kit at all future marathons. Sponsorship is now firmly established in athletics in most countries of the world and just like other sports, athletics would be in serious financial trouble without sponsorship. In this New York City Marathon the principal sponsor was the New York Times, which along with numerous other sponsors involved in the wheelchair races and junior races and umpteen other events of the day, which all add up to making the New York City Marathon a unique occasion.

Concerning the prize money, a professional athlete might win by competing in marathons, I say good luck to them and I'm sure that if I was good enough I have no hesitation in saying that I would be doing exactly the same. What I sometimes find hard to stomach though is that marathons wherever staged in the world are usually big fundraising events and as I've written before thousands of pounds are raised by marathon runners who will often do something quite extraordinary in order to get people to sponsor them (like walking backwards for twenty-six miles). The wonderful effort by fundraisers to raise sometimes colossal mounts of money for different charities is a tremendous effort by them. Some of them may well have terminal illnesses and so often at the rear of any marathon there can be thousands of fundraisers running for their favourite charity. Yet at the front of all marathons are the professional runners battling it out amongst themselves as to who will be the eventual winner. The New York City Marathon, just like other marathons, serves a dual purpose where thousands of pounds are collected in by the fundraisers and thousands of pounds are being taken out from the sport by the professional runners. This happens to infuriate me at times but I do realise that the sport would not be the same without the professionals and I do also realise that marathons wherever staged would definitely not be the same without sponsorship.

There was one place I was determined to visit while I was in New York and Nick accompanied me on a visit to the site of the World Trade Centre where, of course, the twin towers once stood and which is now known as Ground Zero. I was now going on a journey into the unknown and I must admit I was drawn out of curiosity to this derelict site in Lower Manhattan. It was also a journey to hell and back. But most importantly it was a journey that everyone in the free world should try to make and see where democracy has been so savagely and mercilessly threatened by fanatical terrorists. I must admit I wasn't sure how I would react and I did visit Ground Zero where such incredible evil took place with gross misgivings bordering on apprehension because it was as though a part of me so assuredly wanted to see it and being in New York it was the ideal opportunity, but another part of me had grave misgivings and I really was in some degree of nervousness because of uncertain doubts which were constantly with me

as to whether I really did want to visit an area where
literally thousands of innocent people had been so brutally
murdered in such an act of blasphemous wickedness.

Ground Zero is surrounded by high, wooden
hoardings which are spread over an area of about sixteen
acres. As some of those hoardings were well above our
height we didn't particularly get a good view of it.
Eventually we did manage to find one of the entrances to
the site and from there we saw the most ghastly view of
mammoth magnitude within our sights. I do not think any
words from me would adequately seem appropriate but I
will at least try and describe my innermost feelings as I
looked at a smouldering wreckage of terrible and awesome
destruction. It was not unlike scenes reminiscent of what
London and other British cities would have experienced
during the blitz and the dark days of the Second World War.
Ground Zero is a bombed site of appalling destruction and
standing at that entrance there was literally no escape that
something horrendous had taken place there just over six
weeks before. My feelings were, to say the least, of gloom
and despondency on a gigantic scale as demolition and
excavation workers worked around the clock to clear away
enormous amounts of rubble consisting of mangled steel
and concrete with still the odd body being found, but
thoughts of finding anyone alive had long since
disappeared.

On seeing that most cruel and hideous site, my
thoughts invariably thought of man's inhumanity to his
fellow man. Why? Why? Why? I asked myself. Is there
so much hate in the world that thousands of people are
sacrificed in such a heartless and callous way? Ground
Zero provides the conscience of the free world with graphic
evidence of the evil there is within it. Ground Zero
demonstrates to me that we must jealously guard our
democratic rights where nations have fought world wars to

Taken from Liberty Island, shows the Twin Towers of the World Trade Centre before both collapsed following a terrorist attack.

The magnificent Manhattan skyline before the fall of the Twin Towers.

A really horrific photograph - a hijacked commercial plane approaches the World Trade Centre seconds before crashing into the North Tower. The South Tower has already been hit by an aircraft.

The Twin Towers billow smoke after both towers had been hit by hijacked airliners.

A picture taken a further distance away after both Towers had collapsed.

This photograph taken from behind the Statue of Liberty as seen from Jersey City, New Jersey after the fall of the Twin Towers.

A truck sits in the rubble of the Twin Towers.

Traffic clogs the streets of Manhattan after the terrorist attack.

Taken the day after the collapse of the Twin Towers on 12th September 2001, and at Ground Zero the search is on for survivors.

The flag of the Stars and Stripes at half mast, taken a few days after September 11th. To the left of the flag the Empire State Building and to the right the Chrysler Building.

preserve and as I stared out on the sheer hopelessness at what I was seeing, I couldn't help but think for a few fleeting moments of what the IRA have tried to achieve in Great Britain. By targeting certain areas with unexploded bombs left near buildings in city centres, only by some miracle of miracles more innocent victims haven't been killed. Could it really be that it was the IRA's intention over the years to do something similar and as sinister and so wretchedly wicked in my country as I continued to transfix my eyes on something so grotesque that it will always be with me. All democratic countries in the world must realise that what has happened at Ground Zero is a threat to the whole of civilisation as we in the Western world know it. Terrorists do not believe in democracy because they deliberately target innocent civilians and only cowards could act in such a way when they flattened the World Trade Centre. I also believe you should never negotiate with terrorists whoever and wherever they may be. How could the West possibly negotiate with Bin Laden of all people? The President of the United States had said the perpetrators must be hunted down and on seeing Ground Zero with my very own eyes I've never seen a more cowardly act of ponderous proportion and it was in this area of Lower Manhattan in an empty shop window I saw a poster with a picture of the most wanted man on earth. It read "Wanted dead or alive Osama Bin Laden for mass murder in New York City".

Conversation with Nick seemed to have dried up as we looked out on a bombed site in an area previously known as the World Trade Centre. This was I believe because it leaves one with a numb feeling just looking at it. One can be lost for words as one contemplates the awful events of that day where nearly a hundred of my fellow British citizens had perished. While there I did try to visualise what the last moments of those killed would be.

Try to imagine the last moments of those killed who were passengers on the two hijacked planes as in desperation and in such a distressed state tried to make contact with loved ones on mobile phones before those planes crashed into the Twin Towers. The predicament of the office workers and business people in the Twin Towers as they fought amongst the fire, smoke and debris, and eventually realising there was no escape and some of them finally having to jump to their deaths because the heat and smoke was so intense and unbearable. What their last thoughts would be God only knows. The so brave New York Fire Fighters, all three hundred and forty-three of them and twenty-three Police Officers who were inside or near the Twin Towers. Heroes all as the massive jungle of tangled wreckage came crashing down. What chance did those poor people have? I can actually feel ill just thinking about it. The lives of relatives, of loved ones who perished that day have been irrevocably shattered forever and on September 11th over five thousand children lost a parent. That massive loss of life means that many families will never recover and the hurt I felt at Ground Zero that day was very real indeed.

Before leaving the vicinity of Ground Zero there was the most unpleasant of smells like a cloud hanging over the area. One can smell it all around the deserted streets in that part of Lower Manhattan, it being a sort of acid, smoky and dust smell which if one stays in the area long enough the smell seems to cling to the throat. I'm sure that what came hurtling down from the skies that day leaving such a smouldering wreckage of enormous proportions, that the smell from that wreckage will continue to be in the air for some time to come. The devastation was not just confined to the site of Ground Zero because in that part of Lower Manhattan many of the streets are virtually deserted. Where once prosperous businesses flourished, businesses have all but closed down and many shops boarded up. Even the fashionable restaurants have had to close. The skyscrapers near Ground Zero are also near empty as office workers have been moved to temporary buildings. The whole area has now a ghostly feel about it with the very heart of the city having been ripped away. It means also that the thousands of office workers who worked at the Twin Towers are no more, not forgetting also the many business people who would fly in from various parts of the world to attend business meetings at the World Trade Centre. At present no business is being done near that part of Lower Manhattan, consequently all businesses have suffered as a result. Even the taxi driver who took Nick and I to Ground Zero that day told us that when the tragedy struck he lost nearly three quarters of his regular customers, "Nearly all my taxi business was done by picking up people at airports and transporting them to the World Trade Centre. Of course, all that is now finished. I nearly went bankrupt and times are still very difficult" he said.

On leaving Ground Zero it was most noticeable that many people had left bunches of flowers with messages pinned to those hoardings. Also another poignant reminder was the messages of sympathy being displayed in empty shop windows on those deserted streets with often a photograph displayed of a loved one missing. The New Yorkers I spoke to during my brief visit to their city were most emphatic by saying that New York would never be the same city again. This catastrophe has hit them hard although Mayor Rudy Giuliani with his enthusiasm and determination is desperately trying to keep their spirits up by encouraging New Yorkers to carry on flying, keep working, go shopping and attend theatres and restaurants as if nothing had ever happened. But the reality of the atrocity on an apocalyptic scale wrought in Lower

Manhattan won't easily go away. I was pleased that I had made the effort to visit Ground Zero and the awesomeness of that sixteen acres bombed site is something one can only experience in person, where man's inhumanity to his fellow man is so blatantly obvious.

Having just mentioned the name of the Mayor of New York, Rudy Giuliani, it is a name on everyone's lips as he is constantly being spoken about. He has emerged as a folk hero in the city and one cannot go far without hearing his name, television, newspapers, the general public, his name is everywhere and there's no escaping from this legendary figure. It has to be said that before September 11th his name would hardly have been known outside his native New York and certainly not in Great Britain but that has now been dramatically changed. Here is a man who has been magnificent in the way he responded to the city's need at surely its most difficult time which would have put the fear of God into lesser men. If ever a city needed strong leadership it so assuredly found it in Rudolph Guiliani. He had supreme qualities of authority, determination and enthusiasm. With his leadership so inspiring and instinctive as an atrocity of horrific proportion unfolded, who can forget him surveying the scene of total destruction and devastation as he stood amongst the smouldering wreckage of the once proud Twin Towers? It was him more than any other human being who held together a frightened and bewildered city. This man was seen everywhere in the city as he faced up to the ultimate challenge of his life and never once shirking his awesome responsibilities. He had to get the city back to some sort of normality and considering the enormity of the atrocity was virtually impossible. He had to order the massive clearance of probably two million tons of rubble, and somehow to inspire the flagging New York City Fire Department and the City's Police Force who had been so cruelly deprived. He visited the relatives of the dead and the injured in hospitals and the funerals he went to must have seemed endless. There is talk of this hero of New York receiving an Honorary Knighthood from the Queen and as nearly a hundred British subjects were killed on September 11th, no American deserves it more.

Before I leave the subject of Rudy Giuliani, it was him more than anyone else in New York who has reduced crime since 1994 by an incredible 62% by waging a zero tolerance style war on crime he has made New York a safer place. He took back the streets from the vandals and the predators and generally unshackled the police from so much red tape in order to get them out on the streets. Consequently, murders, burglary, rapes, muggings and drug pushers in the five boroughs of New York have been reduced significantly. The population of New York and London are very similar but there's nearly twice as many police in New York. Surely there's a lesson here for British politicians, if any would listen that is, as crime in many British cities is escalating out of control. Zero tolerance works in New York so why can't it work in Britain? My country could learn much from Rudy Guiliani because I believe successive British Governments have failed dismally in recent years as crime figures are soaring. Britain must not be too proud to ask New York how they have done it. My answer would be send for Rudy Guiliani.

Being in New York when America was at war I felt I had to some extent a grandstand view of the proceedings so far. Not only were the newspapers full of the war but the television network repeatedly went over the events of September 11th and the repercussion of that day. In fact, one channel seemed to talk of nothing else as politicians and ordinary New Yorkers were forever being interviewed and the retaliation by American and British air strikes on Afghanistan had received universal approval throughout

America, particularly when it was known that the Taliban were being bombed, but like many wars often the innocent were killed and what was distressing was those terrifying rockets hitting the wrong targets as the innocent were slaughtered. But the top priority for all Americans was to find the terrorist Bin Laden and his Al Queda fighters. America wouldn't rest until he was caught dead or alive and in a shop in Fifth Avenue toilet rolls were even being sold with the hated Bin Laden's picture with the dead or alive words stamped on every single sheet of toilet paper.

According to the Americans, the President, George W Bush, has grown in stature since the outbreak of the war and I would say about 90% of the Americans support him. His actions seemed to have been purposeful and decisive which all the country would expect from its President but who would envy his awesome responsibilities as leader of the free world where he can give an order and unleash those horrifying rockets knowing that many innocent people will be killed? Recently America has developed a 15,000-lb. fuel air explosion bomb which has been dropped on Taliban positions. The weapon is known as a "daisy cutter" and can cause intolerable damage and for me being an ex soldier it doesn't take too much of the imagination to realise that the name of "daisy cutter" automatically makes me think of scorched earth as weapons become progressively worse with the advent of time. The Americans though want the war over as quickly as possible according to the media. The Bush administration is becoming increasingly concerned that public opinion abroad may be turning against the American military in Afghanistan. This hurts America which I think is justly sensitive to criticism as only Great Britain it seems at present is openly supporting its greatest ally in combating terrorism.

Tony Blair's newfound enthusiasm for combating terrorism causes me concern. A few days after September

11th the Prime Minister informed the British people that terrorism must be defeated. If he's so serious about defeating terrorism why is it that he seems to have lost interest in the Omagh bombing in Northern Ireland, where nearly four years ago 29 innocent people were so cruelly murdered by known terrorists and hundreds maimed and disfigured. Now only because of a long running campaign by the *Daily Mail* to bring those people responsible to justice has the outrageous atrocity not been allowed to be forgotten, so what's the difference between an Irish terrorist and an international one? Surely a terrorist is a terrorist wherever they may be and should not be treated differently.

Also on television and another subject that wouldn't go away was the anthrax scare which was sweeping the country. There was no doubt that America was frightened because anthrax is a highly infectious bacterial disease which usually affects animals, notably cattle and sheep which can in some instances be transmitted to human-beings. The fear was understandable because up to when I arrived in the States five Americans had been contaminated with the disease and had died, including one New Yorker with literally thousands of people being put on antibiotics. All this had happened since September 11th and at first it was thought that Bin Laden was the Chief Instigator of these deaths as suspicious letters began arriving at many offices throughout America. The letters were laced with anthrax spores which is in the form of a powder that will float in the air and infect the lungs once the letter has been opened, and can be a killer which has evidently proved to be the case.

It is now thought that a serial killer is on the loose and has become the main suspect and nearly four months later from the first anthrax letter the sender has yet to be caught. So seriously did America view these anthrax scares that the F.B.I. was called in and so far their investigation has had little success in capturing the culprit. Frustrated at their inability to achieve a breakthrough, the F.B.I. is dealing with a case which is quite unparalleled in America, by trying to track a killer who is sending those deadly spores through the post, who also has a grudge against America because of what is written in those anthrax letters. At present all is quiet but I'm sure that all America is holding its breath as to whether he or she strikes again.

"Who is David Beckham?" answered the tour guide in answer to my question. Nick and I were with a group being taken on a tour of the most famous sports arena and concert stadium in New York and the guided tour was taking place at the Madison Square Garden. It really is the most celebrated concert and sports venue with only the very top in show business performing there. Among the sports played there are basketball and ice hockey. Many championship boxing matches have been staged there and I still have distant boyhood memories of world titled boxing bouts being broadcast over the wireless from New York. Because of those memories, Madison Square Garden always had an air of magical mystery about it for me, never thinking that one day I would be taken on an all access tour to every part of the building where over six hundred different events take place every year. This magnificent venue on this behind the scenes tour really does have the most fabulous facilities of any similar arena or stadium anywhere.

So it was in the locker rooms of Madison Square Garden where these famous players of basketball and ice hockey change that I asked the tour guide if he had heard of David Beckham. He had gone on endlessly about the legendary status of super stars who play these two sports that, out of curiosity, I asked him about Beckham. Now David Beckham must surely be the most well known personality in Great Britain today. Even if you do not know a thing about soccer, you must have heard of him but in the locker room (changing room in the UK) the tour guide hadn't got a clue as to who David Beckham was. I mention this short story because although some soccer is played in the States, it is still a relatively minor sport across America. The Americans are so deeply entrenched in their traditional sports like baseball, American football, basketball and ice hockey, so the name of David Beckham would be of little consequence in the States whereas in Britain he is idolised by being known as the greatest soccer player of his generation. Strange that on speaking the same language, often with strong family links, and have even fought world wars together, and have this so-called special relationship between our two countries, that soccer is not a major sport in America and because of that the Americans will continue to ask "Who is David Beckham?"

My last morning in New York and after shopping in the vicinity of the Wellington Hotel and another look inside Central Park and with Nick for company we had arranged a behind the scenes tour of a quite majestic theatre known as Carnegie Hall, situated on 57th Avenue just off 5th Avenue. It is one of the oldest theatres in New York and is well steeped in the traditions of music. It is owned by the City of New York which contributes public funds to its maintenance and improvement. Like Madison Square Garden all the celebrities of the music world have appeared there and in the forthcoming weeks leading up to Christmas the Boston Symphony Orchestra, the New York Pops Orchestra and the equally famous Philadelphia Orchestra will all be appearing there. The Rose Museum was of particular interest to me, not just because of the music personalities and orchestras who have appeared there, but how this so beautiful old music hall was built when there was an escalation of tall buildings being built throughout the city. I would simply have loved to have sat in the very special atmosphere of Carnegie Hall and to have witnessed a live show there, like one of those famous orchestras mentioned. Perhaps I can make it another time.

"Give my regards to Broadway". Yes, I've been there and so many other places too during my two short stays in the city. New York really does generate intense excitement of an uncontrollable nature. It displays many contrary moods as one tries to touch the soul of the city, New York being the centre for shipping, for transportation, for communication, for finance, for fashion, for shopping, for entertainment and so much more. New York is a voyage of discovery and I'm sure that if I were to visit the city a hundred times I would always have this feeling of discovery. My visit for the marathon was pulsating from start to finish. I squeezed so much in during just a few days and writing this book means that I have some really momentous memories of the Big Apple and by competing in the marathon and seeing the horrors of Ground Zero I feel I have a close affinity with the place. Yet virtually all my life which includes New York, I had no wish whatsoever to visit America. I actually had the mistaken impression that Americans would be too brash and loud for me to even begin to contemplate. How wrong can one be for it was in Boston, Massachusetts, that I was rather pleasantly surprised by the courtesy and good manners of the people there which has now, I'm pleased to say, been extended to the good citizens of New York. The Yanks have this marvellous saying after being in conversation with them "have a nice day", which I believe is said with sincerity. I also believe the average American is genuinely proud to be an American, proud of what their country has achieved during its comparatively short history, and the land of freedom and liberty just so happens to be the most powerful nation on earth and they are proud of that too.

So it was that in the Wellington Hotel I shook hands

for the last time with Nick Wright. His plane was taking off from Newark Airport an hour earlier than my flight, which was from the John F Kennedy Airport. He was not only a good room-mate but a friend also and I like to think he valued his friendship with me as much as I did with him and on saying my goodbyes to other marathoners in the hotel, I made my way by the laid-on bus to the airport for the 4 pm flight to Heathrow. A last glance of Manhattan with its glittering streets which seemed as usual to be overflowing with shoppers on the pavements, and out on the streets amongst such a high congestion of traffic, the familiar yellow cabs, and evidently there are 14,000 of them in the city, with their often impatient drivers as they dive in and out of constant traffic jams which any racing driver would be proud of, and the huge skyscrapers looking down on a vast metropolis. But reaching above all it surveys is the towering and majestic Empire State Building and once again the highest building in New York which has come about by the most terrible consequences imaginable.

On the hour-long drive to the airport it was most noticeable that the American flag could be seen flying in many neighbourhoods. I'm also sure it is a form of patriotism rarely seen in the States before and I'm sure that since September 11th has made many Americans take a good look at themselves and are reaching out for this patriotism as never before, at a time of crisis people generally do pull together and Americans need each other now more than ever. I can think back to my childhood days of growing up during the Second World War years and the comradeship of people towards each other was marvellous and far greater than today. People really would go out of their way to help one another and this is the spirit and I believe the attitude the Americans are experiencing at this present time. Yes America is extremely patriotic right now and the flag of the Stars and Stripes proves exactly that, particularly in New York.

If the Americans are serious about defeating terrorism in future they must tighten up security against fanatical hijackers at their airports because the security at the John F Kennedy Airport left a lot to be desired. I would have thought that what happened in New York just over six weeks before that all airports would be very security conscious. Normally one might go through several check-points before one is allowed on a plane. At least at one check point one will be searched by Security Officers who with a scanner (metal detector) will place the scanner on various parts of the body. The scanner will then bleep if any metallic substance is found. As my pockets were half full with loose change at the time, not once was I asked to display what I had in my pockets, even when the scanner bleeped. Also, in order that I wouldn't lose my marathon (metal) medal, I deliberately hung it around my neck under my shirt. When the scanner bleeped when it reached my medal, I was never asked what was under my shirt. I could have been carrying something far more dangerous on my body like some explosive device and could well have been allowed to board the plane. Yet at Heathrow Airport when I left the UK, I was scrupulously searched and quite rightly asked to display everything I was carrying. I have read recently that security at American airports has tightened up considerably and from what I saw at the John F Kennedy Airport it needed to.

Less than half an hour into my flight home I immediately became dreadfully tired, so tired was I that I should have had little difficulty in sleeping, and I knew that the tiredness I was experiencing was a belated tiredness from the marathon which had finally caught up with me. This can certainly be the case as tiredness will often strike two or three days after a marathon but I was not being allowed the opportunity to sleep because of the persistent pain I was encountering from my ankle. I naturally assumed it was the rarefied air from being inside the aircraft as my right leg from below the knee to the ankle ballooned up quite alarmingly which was obviously causing me much concern. So for most of the time spent in the plane I was so desperately tired but literally unable to sleep as I found myself continually walking up and down those aisles on the plane because every time I sat down the pain seemed to increase and I was also very aware that blood clots can appear during long flights which can cause serious complications. It was vitally important, therefore, to keep moving as I dragged my aching body along those aisles. I was not sure what my fellow passengers thought because they must have been aware of me constantly on the move and it was a very relieved man indeed when the aircraft finally touched down at Heathrow Airport after a flight of nearly seven hours. By this time I was genuinely concerned that I may have put excessive pressure on my ankle while completing the marathon (which proved to be the case as I've recently had an operation on it and I dread to think that my marathon days are maybe over) and in my stubbornness and my burning desire to complete the marathon, my wife's prediction was correct when she had said that two marathons in one year was too much for me.

On the train journey home I was still in a state of high excitement at having completed the marathon and I couldn't quite comprehend that within five days I had flown to America and whetted my appetite for New York once more, completed the Big Apple marathon, all twenty-six miles of it, had seen the unspeakable horrors of Ground Zero and here I was nearly home again and I found it extremely difficult to believe what had happened in just a few days but the memories of "Autumn in New York" was a constant reminder to me that it actually did happen and I had achieved my ambition of completing that marathon.

The feelings of elation just wouldn't go away. It was even more satisfying because I will always consider it the toughest of all marathons I have ever participated in. I had encountered many obstacles as I struggled to keep the momentum going.

Say, for example, I had dropped out through exhaustion or an injury, which was always a distinct possibility, I would have been inconsolable in my disappointment. How would I have coped with the embarrassment of failure as I wouldn't have been able to collect a single penny of sponsorship money and any money previously collected would be subsequently returned to my sponsors. It would have meant the "Get Kids Going" charity would have received absolutely nothing from me. Fortunately, that situation never arose and that's why it was so imperative I completed the marathon, otherwise I would have felt I'd let so many people down. But as I come to the end of this book there is just one person who I would like to thank above all others, and I'm not forgetting the fantastic encouragement I received from countless New Yorkers on the marathon route and also not forgetting the generosity of those people who sponsored me, Edna stayed permanently in my thoughts as I thought of her massive disabilities with a body so pitifully ravaged by Motor Neurone Disease, she being once again my inspiration during at times a most gruelling race. When my concentration wavered she, without knowing it, relentlessly spurred me on. It's quite possible I couldn't have done it without thinking of her. Also, if this book is successful, then the proceeds from the sale of the book will jointly go to the "Get Kids Going" charity and to the Mayor of New York's fund for relatives of loved ones lost on September 11th. I realise I've been so incredibly fortunate in my life and I appreciate others in this world have not been so lucky and I shall always be eternally grateful that I was fit enough and well enough to go to New York and successfully complete the marathon there.

It was a visibly tired husband that my wife greeted at Peterborough railway station. We then travelled by car for the short journey home to Market Deeping. There's no skyscrapers or yellow cabs here, and the permanent traffic noise of Fifth Avenue, which interrupted so many hours of precious sleep, would soon be a distant memory, and I was back in England again. My England, I had returned from the country of the Stars and Stripes to the Union Jack of rural middle England, and where Manhattan would seem a billion miles away. I must admit though to being totally exhausted as I so very much needed sleep, and it would have been absolute heaven to have slept for a whole week, particularly as I would at last be in my own bed and after those few stimulating and quite pulsating days in New York I was definitely ready for my bed. I also know that the peacefulness of dear old Market Deeping would be blissful in comparison to where I'd returned from. So I was nearly home with lots to tell my grandchildren about. Could I really put into words by trying to explain to them the exhilaration and unimaginable joy I experienced when I hit that finish line in Central Park. Perhaps with the advancing years the memories of an Autumn day in the United States of America will gradually fade and when I'm really old and grumpy and unbearable to live with and nobody will believe the rantings of a rather pathetic old man who mumbles on endlessly about a very special day in New York. I shall then provide the evidence for all to see, the 2001 New York City Marathon medal and yes, I really did do it.

The Ultimate Prize
The 2001 New York City Marathon Medal

The Author with Nick Wright from Bristol outside the entrance to Central Park on Central Park South.

The messages of sympathy being displayed in empty shop windows near where the Twin Towers stood.

The author on visiting the finish line area the morning after the Marathon in Central Park.

The author also at the finish area of the Marathon with the statue of Co-Founder and rack director Fred Lebow who died in 1994.

The author at one of the entrances to the site of the former World Trade Centre now known as Ground Zero.

Six months later.
With the Empire State Building in the foreground, two columns of light representing the Twin Towers are beamed skyward from Ground Zero in a memorial called 'The Tribute in Light' to commemorate the 6th month anniversary of the attack on the World Trade Centre.